High Voltage Women

High Voltage Women

Breaking Barriers at Seattle City Light

Ellie Belew

RED LETTER PRESS • Seattle

Red Letter Press
4710 University Way NE, Suite 100
Seattle, WA 98105 • (206)985-4621
RLP@redletterpress.org
www.RedLetterPress.org

FIRST EDITION 2019
ISBN 978-0-932323-34-7

Cover and book design: Helen Gilbert
Cover photo: Heidi Durham, 1977 by Marcel Hatch/*Freedom Socialist*

"The Trade Experience," by Joanne Ward © 2012. Used with permission.

"The Ballad of Clara Fraser," by Patrick Haggerty © 1979. Used with permission.

Library of Congress Cataloging-in-Publication Data

Names: Belew, Ellie, author.
Title: High voltage women : breaking barriers at Seattle City Light / Ellie Belew.
Description: First edition. | Seattle, WA : Red Letter Press, [2019] | Includes bibliographical references and index.
Identifiers: LCCN 2018049501 | ISBN 9780932323347 (alk. paper)
Subjects: LCSH: Seattle City Light--Employees--History. | Women electric industry workers--Washington (State)--Seattle--History. | Sex discrimination in employment--Washington (State)--Seattle--History. | Affirmative action programs--Washington (State)--Seattle--History.
Classification: LCC HD9685.U7 S4334 2019 | DDC 331.4/8213192409797772--dc23
LC record available at https://lccn.loc.gov/2018049501

Red Letter Press is grateful to all the contributors, large and small,
who helped make this book possible,
with special thanks to the major organizational donors—
International Brotherhood of Electrical Workers, Local #77,
Freedom Socialist Party,
Librarians' Guild, Local #2626 AFSCME (Los Angeles),
Radical Women,
Washington Women in Trades
—and the courageous front-runner tradeswomen
who lived the story.

Contents

Author's Preface

By Ellie Belew

Red Letter Press asked me, as an autonomous historian, to document the history of the ten women who went through Seattle City Light's Electrical Trades Trainee (ETT) program, and the program itself, including its designer and director, Clara Fraser.

The more information I gathered and organized for this book, the more I came to appreciate the sheer tenacity of these women— their desire and insistence throughout all their struggles, not just for equality but for equity.

It is almost inconceivable, some 45 years later, to appreciate how unyielding these women were. The ETTs persevered, learning a multitude of difficult and unfamiliar skills while enduring an almost daily mix of harassment, slurs, innuendos, and sometimes illegal workplace practices. Socialist feminist Clara Fraser came to City Light after years of organizing, rallying, and training workers. She brought a practical vision for a successful women's ETT program within a publicly owned utility and was not about to let anyone, including the powers-that-be, block this program or the social reforms it would deliver.

Power over the ETT program initially lay with City Light Superintendent Gordon Vickery; with Seattle Mayor Uhlman; and to some degree, with IBEW #77, the union representing City Light's electrical trade workers, including the ETTs. Less obvious, but ultimately more powerful than any of these, were the cumulative efforts of the ETTs, Fraser, the Freedom Socialist Party, Radical Women, and ever-increasing public support for affirmative action at City Light and the City of Seattle.

Stakes were high for all parties involved, but ultimately the ten ETTs were the program. They were considered by many to embody the success or failure of the program, their personal accomplishments were ascribed to the program, while they were individually and collectively the target for opposition to the program itself. In the face of endless challenges and defeats, these women refused to give up. Two left for other work before the ETTs won the discrimination complaint that reinstated their jobs. Two were seriously injured on the job. All struggled to advance according to their abilities.

Such heroism is often portrayed simplistically, with evil-to-the-core villains and faultless heroes. (Heroines are rare.) In this book, the heroines (and some heroes) are just like you, like your co-workers, your neighbors, your friends. They faced the same or greater risks as you will, when you step up. Their stories are a testament to what can be changed, and what it takes to do so.

Our work is before us. I second the words of Clara Fraser:

> And what better fate can a person carve out than participation in the emancipation of humanity? What better use to make of one's life than in preparing that new civilization? We look toward a time when we shall have ceased to mourn martyrs. A time when we are no longer occupied with explaining defeats and rising above betrayal. Not because we will have forgotten the past, but simply because we are so engrossed and fulfilled in the role of creating a world rich with freedom, plenty, humane relations between people, and the joy of living.[1]

–April 2018

Introduction

By Megan Cornish

There are milestones that reward all the struggles we women had to get into our trades.

Like the distinct sense of accomplishment when you pass an electrical pole or a vault or a piece of substation equipment and think, "I helped build that." Like the special moment when you realize that crew chiefs meeting with you to arrange outages are treating you with the same respect as your male co-workers.

One of my treasured memories is when, early in my career at Seattle City Light, an older white journey-level worker confided to me how his attitude had changed toward men of color and women electricians because of their positive influence in making the union stronger and more militant.

But there is also a price that we advance troops paid—both those who were forced out and those who stayed. Many of the personal stories in this book describe this cost. Heidi Durham, who broke her back in an on-the-job accident and suffered early onset Alzheimer's disease, paid the hardest. Yet she was also a dynamic organizer and leader for many years, embodying the rewards of fighting the good fight in a rich but too brief life.

This book is a close-up of a drama enacted nationally by women who risked heartache to seek the simple pleasures—and higher paychecks—that come with careers in construction trades and other "male" jobs. Huge thanks to Ellie Belew for telling this history from the authentic perspective of the pioneers—and radicals—who too often get written out of "official" narratives. According to establishment pundits, integration into trades in the 1970s happened because society somehow just got enlightened and opened the doors of opportunity. Well, no. It was a hard-fought battle. Those doors were forced open with pry bars!

This book not only shows that you can fight misogynist institutions, it's an essential guide on how to do it. As in the Black civil rights movement, which made affirmative action measures like the Electrical Trades Trainee program possible, the elements of success were militant leadership, a cohesive group of fighters, and community support.

Clara Fraser, the architect of and mentor to Seattle City Light's Electrical Trades Trainee (ETT) program for women, taught us the lessons of her long history of radical organizing and building working-class solidarity. She participated in a union drive at a big Chicago department store during WWII. Later she was an assembly-line electrician at Boeing in Seattle and, during the long strike of 1948, helped organize a stroller brigade of mothers and babies in defiance of an anti-picketing injunction. She was arrested in 1969 while supporting a strike of women photo-finishers and won vindication in court. In 1971, after an arrest when police raided a benefit for the antiwar Seattle Seven defendants, she successfully defended herself in court (going on to teach the popular "Women's Legal Self-Defense" class series). During this period, she worked in various parts of the federal anti-poverty program, becoming an ace trainer who helped men and women of color gain vital job skills. She wrote on the inseparability of the "race question," the "woman question," and the class struggle as early as 1965.

No surprise then that the groups she helped form, Radical Women (RW) and the Freedom Socialist Party (FSP), were also in the forefront in recognizing these interconnected issues. We organized with the Black Panther Party and defended them in the streets. We supported the battles waged by the United Construction Workers Association for hiring people of color. Our members, including me, were arrested with them in civil disobedience actions. We worked with Black women from the anti-poverty program to launch the first demonstration for legalized abortion in Washington State. We defended Native American fishing rights and occupations, supported farmworkers, marched against the Vietnam War, and helped organize the first staff strike at the University of Washington. We were in the leadership of some of the first lesbian/gay marches in Seattle. Radical Women members became truck drivers, welders, firefighters, phone installers and bus drivers. For a handful of women, we broke into a hell of a lot of trades!

I moved into Clara's highly political collective household soon after joining Radical Women. During the City Light walkout that exploded right before the ETTs started work, I had the thrilling experience of hearing about each day's events and listening to her plot strategy in evening phone conversations with co-workers.

That was the background for the battle by Radical Women members Heidi Durham, Teri Bach and me to become high-voltage electricians at City Light.

And it was a battle. If we and other ETTs had not fought together against City Light management, all or most of us would've been gone in short order, and few other women would have followed. The doors would have been closed, even to those women who came along later and distanced themselves from those of us they called "troublemakers." Instead, our activism and on-the-job persistence had a ripple effect on public and private employment in the whole area.

It can't be emphasized enough that structural racism and sexism have always made it doubly hard for women of color to get in and stay in non-traditional trades and occupations. Until they get equal access, no one's gains can be lasting. RW members went to public hearing after public hearing calling on the city to set up a separate category and hiring goals for women of color, because they were—and still are—being left out.

It was the economic double-jeopardy of sexism and racism that forced Daisy Jones, a Black woman and the most seasoned leader among the ETTs, to quit the program for a lower-paid job before we were actually laid off. She had to support her children. But this meant she automatically lost the ability to return to the utility when the ETTs won our discrimination case.

Job fairness and pay equity are fundamental class issues. Racism and sexism are so embedded in this country that they have severely weakened class consciousness. That's why integrating the workforce is key to building a strong labor movement. We have to demand a bigger "pie" for workers instead of being forced to vie with each other for ever-shrinking pieces.

The RW members at City Light were always clear that any grief that came down on women electricians and men of color was attributable to management. Many of our tormenters on the crews bought their place in management that way.

Let's be clear about this: affirmative action was the only way that men of color and women of any race got into trades. There was no "level playing field" then and there isn't now. When conservatives finally were able to recast affirmative action as somehow unfair to white men, systemic racism and sexism slammed the doors to jobs and education almost as tight as they had been in the 1970s. Today, women are only three percent of construction, mining and petroleum workers. Only 12.2 percent in these fields are non-white.

The powers-that-be haven't stopped with chipping away at affirmative action, either. All the social gains won by working people in the 20th century are being rolled back. We will lose them all unless we learn the lessons of working-class solidarity and militancy.

Not everyone who reads this book will want to go into non-traditional trades. But I hope you will be inspired to become feminist activists and, dare I say it, radicals. Even more than when I started working at City Light, these times—when living standards of working people and even life on the planet are at stake—demand no less.

Speaking as a socialist feminist, I'm more convinced now than ever that the most basic demands for equality and a decent life for those who create the wealth of society, will never be won under the profit system. Without systemic change, hard-won reforms can only be retained through a perpetual fight.

Little did I know when I started out at City Light that this job would so much define my life. But I was already hooked on battling for a better world. And the joy, laughter and comradeship of that collective enterprise is its own reward. I recommend it to anyone.

–August 2018

Heidi Durham, Teri Bach and Megan Cornish show off their pole-climbing boots in anticipation of entering the City Light linework apprenticeship.

Abbreviations

BRRC   Bill of Rights and Responsibilities Committee

CERCL   Employee Committee for Equal Rights at City Light

DOL   U.S. Department of Labor

EEO   Equal Employment Opportunity: the principles, objectives and implementation of non-discriminatory workplace practices as overseen by the Equal Employment Opportunity Commission

EEOC   U.S. Equal Employment Opportunity Commission

ETT   Electrical Trades Trainee

FSP   Freedom Socialist Party

HRD   Human Rights Department (Seattle)

IBEW   International Brotherhood of Electrical Workers

OWR   Office of Women's Rights (Seattle)

PSC   Public Service Careers

RW   Radical Women

SCL   Seattle City Light

UCWA   United Construction Workers Association

Key Characters

Angel Arrasmith Electrical Trades Trainee

Teri Bach Electrical Trades Trainee; member of Radical Women (RW) and Freedom Socialist Party (FSP)

Marilyn Bircher (Robeson) Cost Accountant at City Light and employee militant

Carole Coe (Hauskins) Director of Administrative Services at City Light; administrative assistant to the superintendent

Megan Cornish Electrical Trades Trainee; member of RW and FSP

Heidi Durham Electrical Trades Trainee; member of RW and FSP

Clara Fraser Coordinator of Training and Education at City Light; initially in charge of the Electrical Trades Trainee program; a founder and leader of FSP and RW

Jennifer Gordon Electrical Trades Trainee

Daisy Jones (Erhart) Electrical Trades Trainee

Letha Neal (Neal-Gray) Electrical Trades Trainee

Jody Olvera Electrical Trades Trainee

Bill Rheubottom City Light departmental training coordinator; Clara Fraser's supervisor

Charles Royer Seattle mayor from 1978-1989

Charlie Silvernale Longtime officer of IBEW Local #77

Wes Uhlman Seattle mayor from 1969-1977

Gordon Vickery Superintendent of Seattle City Light, 1972-79

Margie Wakenight (Bellinger) Electrical Trades Trainee

Joan Williams Equal Employment Opportunity officer at Seattle City Light

Patty Wong (Eng) Electrical Trades Trainee (the only ETT not to file discrimination charges against City Light)

Construction of the Diablo Dam powerhouse on the Skagit River, Whatcom County, Washington, 1935.

A Time for Transformers

The stage for the first women utility electrical workers at Seattle City Light was set decades before their arrival. The civil rights movement of the late 1950s and early 1960s drew the U.S. public into bold and insistent political action. In response, federal programs for social progress, including affirmative action, were enacted during John F. Kennedy's presidency, in part to quiet such protest. In his acceptance speech at the 1960 Democratic National Convention, Kennedy outlined his vision of what needed to be changed:

> unsolved problems of peace and war, unconquered problems of ignorance and prejudice, unanswered questions of poverty and surplus.[2]

Kennedy's 1961 Executive Order 10925 mandated affirmative action hiring and working conditions "without regard to race, creed, color, or national origin."[3]

Protests against institutionalized racism and other social injustice continued after Kennedy's assassination in 1963. His successor, Lyndon Johnson, responded with his "Great Society" program, which brought changes to education, medical care, urban blight, rural poverty, and transportation systems.

Throughout the United States, those on the political left—progressives, liberals, and radicals—kept pressure on federal and state governments to end the Vietnam War, to make the Civil Rights Act of 1964 a reality, to fight poverty, to establish equal rights for women and LGBTQ people, to legalize abortion, and to protect the environment.

These social and political values clashed at many levels with those of people on the right. What was then called "the Establishment"—the structures and social mechanisms of the military, major industry, finance, and mainstream politics—used its powers to block progress on racism, sexism, poverty, and environmental protections.

Blue-collar workers, especially those in the construction trades, generally aligned themselves with the right. Anti-communism had driven radicals and integrationists out of the labor movement during the Red Scare of the 1950s. Anti-communism was also used to justify U.S. military incursions of the 1960s and 1970s, and many unionists opposed the antiwar movement out of patriotism. Sexism was rampant, even within the leftist and civil rights movements, and many treated the burgeoning women's liberation movement with hostility.

In Seattle, two new political organizations emerged, both focused on mobilizing social protest to change society. The Freedom Socialist Party (FSP) had spun off from the Socialist Workers Party in 1966 over several issues, including gender and race. Radical Women, a socialist feminist group, was formed in 1967 and formally affiliated with the FSP in 1973. In the words of co-founder Gloria Martin, Radical Women's purpose was to

> demonstrate that women could act politically, learn and teach theory, administer an organization, develop indigenous leadership, and focus movement and community attention on the sorely neglected matter of women's rights—*and that women could do this on their own.*[4]

Clara Fraser, key to many events in this book, was a founder of both the FSP and Radical Women. A strong personality, she was described variously by reporters as "big, gutsy, vital"[5] and a "warm Jewish earth momma."[6]

The socialist feminist politics of Radical Women and Freedom Socialist Party emphasized the interconnection of women, class and race. Radical Women had a history in the Pacific Northwest of bringing together women of color, Native Americans, lesbians and gays, women's rights, and labor.

Fraser summarized the groups' overlapping politics in her collection of essays and articles, *Revolution, She Wrote:*

> My organizations, Radical Women and the Freedom Socialist Party, are multi-issue, anti-capitalist, socialist feminists....

We fight on all fronts. We see the interconnections of all the different struggles....and we have a vision of the future.[7]

At this time, the workplace in general had become the site for taking on issues of race and then gender inequality. Federally funded construction projects had created a building boom, boosting the wages of construction workers to new highs, especially in relation to manufacturing jobs. With higher wages and ever-increasing demand for trade workers, the traditional union movement's political power grew. But these traditional unions were not training or hiring non-white or non-male workers.

In 1966, the Washington State Board Against Discrimination found that Washington State's 15 Building Trades unions, repre-senting over 29,000 workers, had only 7 non-white apprentices.[8]

The federal Equal Employment Opportunity Commission (EEOC) had been established in 1965 to address workplace discrimination, administering and sometimes enforcing civil rights laws such as the Civil Rights Act of 1964. Johnson's administration also created a federal program that monitored affirmative action hiring mandates and compliance with construction standards, starting in St. Louis, San Francisco, and Cleveland. By 1967, this had evolved into the Philadelphia Plan

which required that prospective contractors...project the number of nonwhite workers on a jobsite *prior* to being awarded the con-tract. Contracting officers could then evaluate the [hiring] projec-tions along with all other factors in determining to whom the contract should be awarded.[9]

Concurrently, another set of federal mandates addressing urban poverty were implemented. One of these, the Model Cities program (under the federal Department of Housing and Urban Development), targeted racial disenfranchisement, providing funding to cities to

reduce social and economic disadvantages in designated neighbor-hoods, provide maximum training and employment opportunities, and establish health services for residents.[10]

In April 1968, the Seattle City Council unanimously passed Ordinance 96619, which prohibited discriminatory housing sales, rentals, and financing. That same year, the City of Seattle received federal funding for major urban renewal and appointed Walter Hundley, a minister and director of the Central Area Motivation Program (an anti-poverty project), as ad hoc director of Seattle's Model Cities program. Many movement activists worked on projects and programs funded through the Model Cities program, including Clara Fraser, who later oversaw the beginning of Seattle City Light's Electrical Trades Trainee (ETT) program for women.

In addition, a group of business leaders led by Seattle attorney Jim Ellis proposed a program they named Forward Thrust. It focused on transit and infrastructure construction and improvements to address the Puget Sound area's population growth. The following February, King County voters approved seven of 12 proposed Forward Thrust bond propositions, worth $333.9 million.

To incorporate federal funding into Forward Thrust projects, King County and Seattle had to meet federal laws on non-discrimination but, at the time, workers on the multitude of public construction projects springing up throughout the Seattle metro area were virtually all white males. (See Appendix 4, Timeline of Affirmative Action and Anti-Discrimination Laws.)

1968 was also a presidential election year, with Democrat Hubert Humphrey, American Independent and segregationist George Wallace, and Republican Richard Nixon running. Across the United States, much of so-called Middle America, frightened by increasing civil disobedience, protests, and a growing counterculture, rallied under the name "the Silent Majority," a slogan made famous by Nixon in the final weeks of his successful campaign. Once in office, Nixon and his administration began to reverse many of the progressive policies and programs from the Kennedy and Johnson administrations, including Johnson's War on Poverty.

But even as the Nixon administration sought to redesign policy, others within the federal government were enacting and providing funding for Johnson-era programs. One of their challenges was to make the states, municipalities, companies, and employers who

Radical Women co-founder Gloria Martin (standing in center) speaks at a 1969 welfare rights demonstration at the state capitol in Olympia, Washington.

sought federal funding comply with affirmative action and anti-discrimination law. This federal enforcement would push Seattle and other cities toward their own affirmative action and anti-discrimination programs. In Seattle this would eventually include changes at its publicly owned utility, Seattle City Light.

By spring of 1969, Seattle Model Cities Director Walter Hundley was encouraging local Black tradesmen to work together to go after jobs covered by federal construction contracts that required hiring workers of color. In May, the Central Contractors Association (CCA) was formed. Tyree Scott, a charismatic, Black second-generation electrician and former Marine, was elected president of the CCA board. CCA members tried negotiating with both the trade unions and major contractors in the Seattle area but continued to be excluded from their lucrative federal contracts.

In cities across the United States, starting in Philadelphia and then in Chicago and Pittsburgh, African American workers shut down federal construction sites in protest. By late summer of 1969, the CCA also shifted its strategy to direct action.

> Forsaking what they believed to be failed forms of negotiation, the CCA brought every major, federally funded construction site in the city of Seattle to a halt in late August and September of 1969. They did this—as other activists were doing in Pittsburgh, Philadelphia, and Chicago at roughly the same time—by disabling equipment, blocking workers from their jobs, and demanding that federal civil rights law be used to force unions to hire more black workers. The most dramatic actions included running a bulldozer into a large open pit at the University of Washington, and marching [more than] a hundred protesters onto the flight apron of Sea-Tac airport to halt air traffic.[11]

These CCA worksite shutdowns on federally funded construction sites within Seattle held up projects valued at millions of dollars. CCA also filed suit to block federal funding of several projects in Seattle because of hiring discrimination. Then-Governor Dan Evans and King County Executive John Spellman tried to mediate between the CCA and local construction unions, but organized labor would not negotiate. Both the federal Equal Employment Opportunity Commission (EEOC) and the federal Department of Labor (DOL) sent representatives to Seattle, although there is no documentation any action was taken.

When Seattle and King County officials started to move toward enforcing affirmative action, the building trades unions provided forceful opposition. In October 1969, the Voice of Irate Construction Employees (VOICE) mobilized 2,000 Caucasian "hard hats" in a downtown Seattle march protesting "forced" hiring of workers of color. Later that month, 3,000 building trades members held a rally in Olympia against "minority" hiring.

In the midst of this turmoil, Wes Uhlman ran for mayor of Seattle. At 34, Uhlman was the youngest legislator in Washington State at the time. He had worked his way up over four terms to the powerful position of the chair of the House Ways and Means Committee and then served a term in the Senate.[12]

Just before he began his campaign, Uhlman had significantly increased the power of Washington mayors:

> As a state senator, he quietly pushed through legislation in 1969 to transfer critical budget authority to the mayor.[13]

This meant Seattle's next mayor would have much greater autonomy over the millions of dollars that Model Cities and Forward Thrust initiatives were pumping into Seattle projects. Mayoral candidate Uhlman delicately courted both liberal and conservative voters, won, and took office a month early, on December 1, 1969. Then, less than two months later, Seattle was hit with what came to be known as the Boeing Bust.

In just over one year, Boeing's Seattle work force shrank from 103,000 to 49,000 employees. The resulting economic depression and unemployment meant the locally generated portion of city coffers Uhlman now controlled were empty. By the end of 1970, unemployment in Seattle was, at 10.7 percent, the highest in the United States. Meanwhile, the city continued to be the site of numerous protests.

> Demonstrators repeatedly shut down buildings at the UW [University of Washington], clogged downtown streets, packed the courthouse lawn, and (every day for one memorable week in May 1970) occupied the Interstate 5 freeway.[14]

A student strike at the University of Washington protesting the Vietnam War culminated in a march of more than 10,000, from campus to downtown, in addition to stopping traffic on Interstate 5. Radical Women, the three-year-old socialist feminist group, took part in these protests and provided leadership in others, especially around the issues of civil rights and women's liberation.

The CCA continued its worksite protests, but was having internal debates over whether it should serve Black workers or Black contractors.[15] In early 1970, Tyree Scott left the CCA to form the United Construction Workers Association (UCWA), which focused on continued worksite protests against segregated unions. A growing number of Seattle activists supported the UCWA, and sometimes participated in UCWA actions. Megan Cornish and other Radical

1972 United Construction Workers Association march in downtown Seattle.

Women members took part in several UCWA protests. They asked for—and received—UCWA support for allowing women into the trades as well. Cornish was among those arrested in UCWA actions and would later be one of the women hired in Seattle City Light's first apprenticeship program for women.

Seattle's unions continued to refuse all of the various settlements proposed by local elected officials to address illegal discrimination. In response, the federal government made the CCA party to federal-court-ordered implementation of the revised Philadelphia Plan. Two years earlier, Nixon had revised the original Philadelphia Plan to replace racial quotas with "good faith efforts in hiring"[16] and use its affirmative action requirements as

> a political wedge issue which could divide two reliably Democratic
> constituencies: African Americans and organized labor.[17]

In 1970, the U.S. Equal Employment Opportunity Commission signed its first Memorandum of Understanding with the federal Department of Labor. Nixon-appointed DOL Secretary George Schultz then used this interagency agreement to enforce the revised Philadelphia Plan. Labor historian Marc Linder, author of *Wars of Attrition*, also attributes the DOL's interest in going after racist practices in the trade unions as a way to break the union movement while also fragmenting the Democrats' traditional constituency, pitting labor against social progressives.[18]

At any rate, federal enforcement of the revised Philadelphia Plan required "an acceptable affirmative action program" in more trade unions in more cities, and targeted their apprenticeship programs. When the unions did not comply, union locals were placed under federal court injunctions with specific directives on how many non-white apprentices they must admit and when these apprentices should be certified as journey-level workers. The apprenticeship programs of four Seattle unions were put under this court order: Sheet Metal Workers #99, Iron Workers #86, Plumbers and Pipefitters #32, and the International Brotherhood of Electrical Workers #46. The CCA and the UCWA took part in the settlement process, but also continued worksite protests, some of which involved physical confrontations and the destruction of property.

Newly elected Seattle Mayor Uhlman was definitely slammed by the combination of major white-collar unemployment and intense, prolific social protest. Uhlman took cover for a bit and regrouped.

> At the end of that first frustrating year [1970], Wes Uhlman virtually disappeared, hunkering in the political bunker. He proposed no new initiatives and held no news conferences. In fact, he rarely left his office.
>
> Then, when the mayor resurfaced, he had a new plan: He would save the city by streamlining it and turning the welter of city agencies into an efficient bureaucracy.
>
> First, he set about creating a number of new departments—he called them "superagencies"—that would give as much authority as possible to Uhlman and his appointees, mostly enthusiastic young professionals without much civil service experience.[19]

Uhlman worked his regional political connections, especially his connection with Senator Warren Magnuson, then chair of the federal Appropriations Committee, to secure significant federal funding for his superagencies. Uhlman instituted citizen commissions, used Model Cities funding to create Community Service Centers (known as Little City Halls), and created the Office of Management and Budget (OMB). The OMB began to standardize Seattle's departments, their budgets, and their hiring and promotions. In effect, the newly created OMB was Uhlman's mechanism for assuming the fiscal power he had legislated to mayors just before becoming one.

Uhlman continued to make more appointments, including Jack Driscoll as director of Personnel. Driscoll's role then expanded to include head examiner of Seattle's Civil Service Commission and director of its Civil Service Department staff. With these three overlapping positions Driscoll was set up to

> [run] roughshod over civil service and unions to pursue an aggressive affirmative-action program to integrate the city's nearly all-white workforce.[20]

In theory, Uhlman's appointments of Seattle's first Black department heads, as well as the formation of Seattle's Human Rights Department (HRD), charged with investigating discrimination charges and recommending policies and legislation, were designed to integrate Seattle's administration.

In reality, Uhlman was not prepared to bring affirmative action into specific departments. Although the Human Rights Department existed, it was not part of Uhlman's administrative decision-making process. Uhlman instead relied upon Jack Driscoll, head of both the Personnel Department and the Civil Service, to implement EEOC requirements.

In late 1971, Uhlman had the opportunity to replace another department head, the superintendent of Seattle City Light. John M. Nelson had held the position since 1963, and had pursued an old-school style of utility management that collaborated with the Lighting Department's unions and encouraged industrial development and low-cost public power. During the latter part of Nelson's administration he proposed several controversial projects including raising Ross Dam, co-ownership of a coal-fired generating plant in Centralia, and construction of a new nuclear power plant near Deception Pass.

Uhlman didn't want Nelson or his policies. This included Nelson's good relations with the unions representing City Light's engineers and trades workers.

> In December 1971, Nelson announced his retirement when Uhlman declined to renominate him. The *Seattle Times* wrote, "In the present period of power-policy conflict, it is small wonder that Nelson was willing to 'take a walk' from the City Light Superintendency when Uhlman reportedly gave him an opportunity to go out with his head in the air rather than bear a stigma of not being reappointed."[21]

Uhlman wanted a superintendent from outside the utility, one who hadn't come up through the ranks. But Uhlman underestimated the power of City Light's internal culture.

> The first nominee [for Superintendent], R.D. Ford, was not confirmed by the City Council after City Light staff members lobbied against his appointment.[22]

Uhlman then nominated Seattle's recently retired fire chief, Gordon Vickery. Chief Vickery had gained a reputation within Seattle government and the community for his autocratic style and abrasive personality. After ordering a number of top-down worksite changes and a contested recruitment program for firefighters of color, Vickery had retired. Some thought Uhlman hired Vickery to make sure he wouldn't run against Uhlman in the upcoming mayoral election. Uhlman told the *Seattle Times* that Vickery is "one of the finest administrators in Seattle" and "knows the bureaucracy, the system and how to get things done."[23]

On May 31, 1972, Gordon Vickery became the utility's ninth superintendent. What Uhlman didn't realize was that federal mandates, in combination with his own administrative decisions (including appointing Vickery), would create a tempest of discord within the city. Out of this would also come an opportunity for tenacious women to break some of the gender barriers at City Light.

> Shortly after Vickery's appointment, congressional amendments to Title VII of the Civil Rights Act gave the EEOC the power to litigate and removed exemptions for local governments as employers.

In response, Uhlman issued an executive order establishing an affirmative action program for all city departments, including Seattle City Light.

As one of Seattle's departments, City Light had been receiving the same directives to meet EEOC compliance as all the other city departments. But the utility had its own corporate culture. Many who worked for City Light took great pride in their employer and personally identified with its legacy as a publicly owned utility founded by J.D. Ross to serve the community.

Going into the early 1970s, people who worked at City Light, especially its tradesmen, considered themselves to be "part of the City Light family." Linemen and other electrical tradesmen (and they were all men) were members of the International Brotherhood of Electrical Workers (IBEW) Local #77. As such, they usually got their work skills and jobs via the informal "FBI" of organized labor: fathers, brothers, and in-laws. This was part of the same overwhelmingly white, all-male, quasi-hereditary unionism that, at the time, most organized craft unions shared.

And as at many utilities, the pay of all of IBEW #77's electrical workers at City Light was (and is) pegged to that of its lineworkers.

This encouraged solidarity since a contractual injury to a lineworker at City Light was a contractual injury to every other IBEW #77 member at City Light. At the same time, the union was experiencing a generational schism in its membership. The new wave of apprentices, which included some Vietnam veterans, were more open to liberal politics and changing social norms that came into conflict with old-school tradesmen.

Concurrently with Vickery's 1972 appointment as superintendent, City Light instituted its first Electrical Trades Trainee (ETT) program. This program was for men of color, although in reality the program did nothing more than boost them up a hiring list, using what is called "selective certification."

Seattle had approved the use of selective certification in entry-level and promotional hiring in 1971. This allowed for the highest-ranking applicants of a particular racial group, if already eligible for a position, to be placed higher on a list of candidates for hiring. But it didn't give them a job.

In the first City Light ETT program, individual Black and Asian American men were placed in the field, singly. Their ETT training was nothing more than one day of orientation, including a free lunch. Then they were assigned as helpers on a line crew. (A line crew helper assists with on-the-ground tasks needed to support the lineworkers, but may work above ground or on electrical circuits, at the discretion of the crew chief.) Minimal statistics were kept on the outcome of this program. Some of these men did make it as helpers at City Light.

Meanwhile, Superintendent Vickery autocratically and preemptively "cleaned house" at the utility. Many who worked under him, including IBEW #77 members, were insulted at Vickery's contempt for workers and their work, his habit of issuing edicts, and his presumption they were all slackers. Even Vickery supporters saw the conflict. According to Walt Sickler, the supervisor of Overhead Construction at City Light:

> [Vickery] was what everybody deemed as an outsider and of course he was a fireman and we had a difficulty equating what a fireman knew about administering a power company. You think in your own channels that somebody to be your boss has to know what you're doing, but what you have to know is that when you get to a certain level it's more administrative than functional.[24]

Resentment quickly grew within the utility's workforce.

> In just a year on the job, [Vickery] had fired or dismissed hundreds of employees, had others prosecuted for theft, and changed City Light's staffing policies.[25]

Vickery had also received a citywide directive to come up with an effective affirmative action program at City Light, one that better met federal and municipal mandates. With this, Vickery initiated conceptual plans for a new Electrical Trades Trainee (ETT) program, aimed at women.

A dominant feature of the old Seattle City Light administration building was a massive 1958 mosaic mural (detail above) by Northwest woman artist Jean Cory Beall. It is emblazened with a motto that expresses the ideal of publicly owned and managed power: "That Man May Use It Freely as the Air He Breathes; the Waters of the Rivers; the Winds of Heaven," paraphrasing a passage from TRAVAIL by Émile Zola.

First Sparks

On April 11, 1973, Clara Fraser applied to the Personnel Division of Seattle's Department of Lighting for two positions: "Coordinator, Departmental Training" and "Coordinator, Education." (Department of Lighting is the historical name of Seattle City Light.) In her application, Fraser summarized her credentials:

> I am a professional trainer, teacher, and training consultant, having planned and conducted staff training and career development programs for many years, specializing in vocational training, para-professional education, and affirmative action orientation.
>
> For the past six years [since 1967], I have worked in the anti-poverty program and as a private consultant concerned mainly with manpower development and staff advancement. I worked for almost four years at SOIC [Seattle Opportunities Industrialization Center, a federally funded jobs training program], and now, in my position with the Concentrated Employment Program [CEP], I work closely with New Careers and Operation Improvement in the constant effort to design and re-design training programs that are both feasible and fulfilling for the people involved....
>
> Federal cutbacks are causing the planned discontinuation of CEP, and that is why I am submitting my application to you.[26]

A *Seattle Times* reporter would later summarize Fraser's work history in a profile of her, documenting the political blacklisting during the McCarthy Red Scare period that forced her from job to job:

> Ms. Fraser has been employed in human-rights programs since 1967.
>
> Before that, she worked as a fashion copy writer, a cab driver, a printer, a factory worker and a secretary.
>
> After five or six years as a secretary in the office of two psychiatrists, she felt she "had to get out because it was so foreign to my approach to things. I believe in the therapy of human alliance,

in joint action with other people in a common cause and common purpose."[27]

Fraser's work background had a bigger political component than might appear.

SOIC, one of the anti-poverty efforts Fraser referred to in her application, was part of Seattle's Model Cities program, administered by Walter Hundley. She was fired from that job and, until 1971, legally contested her firing on the basis of "sex and political ideology" discrimination. One sure cause for friction was that she and a co-worker had organized an International Women's Day seminar for employees and clients that resulted in a lengthy list of demands for improving women's status at the agency.

Fraser's résumé listed her membership in a number of organizations, including Radical Women and the very recently formed Feminist Coordinating Council (FCC). But knowing post-McCarthy Era anti-communism was still rampant, Fraser did not list her membership in another group she had helped found, the Freedom Socialist Party.

However, Fraser's leftist politics and activism were well-known throughout Seattle and by many within the city's government. Two of her references held positions and appointments relating to affirmative action. Millie Henry was director of the Women's Division at the Office of Human Resources. Lynn Bruner was a leader of the Feminist Coordinating Council with Fraser, also on the Washington State Women's Council, and worked at the U.S. Equal Employment Opportunity Commission. (The EEOC had been involved in investigating discrimination claims brought by Tyree Scott, the Central Contractors Association, and the United Construction Workers Association.)

So those at City Light who were considering hiring Clara Fraser were familiar with both her professional and political reputations. For example, Mike Sharar, who helped interview her for the City Light position, recognized her, having produced various local television programs that included pungent interviews with Fraser at rallies and protests. Many people thought Fraser was actually recruited by

Vickery *because* of her feminist activism and organizing skills, which proved she could get the job done implementing affirmative action.

Fraser was not alone in having her experience as a so-called rabble-rouser count as a plus when a job involved affirmative action and/or community outreach. Successful community organizers have community connections and expect real turnout and real results. In addition, dissent had become more mainstream after the massive protests of the 1960s and the disillusionment that accompanied the televised 1973 Watergate hearings into President Nixon's criminal activities.

Clara Fraser was hired as City Light's training and education coordinator on June 4, 1973. William C. Rheubottom was appointed her immediate supervisor at the same time, as departmental training coordinator. Rheubottom was a Black retired military veteran who had worked for Public Service Careers (PSC), assisting affirmative action trainees at the Fire Department. Together they comprised the newly created Training Division of City Light's Administrative Services Division. (PSC was a Department of Labor/Model Cities program operated by the city Personnel Department.)

Within two weeks of hiring Fraser, City Light Superintendent Gordon Vickery introduced Fraser and Rheubottom to the rest of his staff at a large meeting of managers and supervisors. Vickery invited the two to talk about themselves and their training goals. Fraser later noted that she had immediately begun to talk about affirmative action and feminism, to which Vickery half-jokingly warned her to "watch that agitation."[28] But Fraser had never kowtowed to an administrator's discomfort in advocating for equality, and was not about to start now that she worked at City Light.

Soon, memos outlining a proposed Electrical Trades Trainee (ETT) program for women were circulating around the utility. The superintendent's office, the Training Division, and Public Service Careers began to review the earlier Electrical Trades Trainee program that had been for "disadvantaged" and/or "minority" men.

Richard Burt, the director of PSC, called out one problem with the earlier men's program: "No authority [over the trainees was] given to immediate Supervisors of ETTs." Burt advocated for a training committee that worked with these field supervisors, noting that PSC staff would only provide assistance to such a committee. City Light's Training, Equal Employment Opportunity (EEO), and Personnel offices reviewed the Burt proposal and sent their reactions in a written response to Assistant Superintendent Julian Whaley on September 27, 1973. They recommended

> greater emphasis on the affirmative action, remedial nature of the program; inclusion of women and minorities on the Trainee Committee; increased training, EEO, and Trainee Committee involvement in all stages of the process; modifications in the proposed orientation; and human relations training for supervisors and foremen. They criticized discriminatory aspects of the proposal such as required night classes for the women, the use of the terms "he/his" throughout a program for women, a tone of paternalism toward the trainees, and too much of a "business as usual" underestimation of the unusual and historic nature of the program.[29]

Fraser's boss and head of the utility's Training Division, Bill Rheubottom, sent a memo making it clear that as the new ETT program evolved, it would be a "product of collaboration between PSC and Joan Williams." (Joan Williams, a Black woman, was the City Light employee assigned to oversee issues of job equity as EEO officer. She reported directly to the superintendent, and had been involved with the original ETT program for men of color.)

By September, there was enough buy-in on a women's program to formally assign a program coordinator. Clara Fraser won the job and was put in charge of planning and implementing the program, a landmark project to develop women into utility electrical workers. With that, the committee on the ETT project began to meet. At this point, it included Fraser, Rheubottom, City Light Assistant Superintendent Julian Whaley, and representatives of the city's Personnel and Civil Service departments.

The new ETT program began to take shape as the planning committee's members sketched out orientation for incoming trainees, as well as how to provide schooling on electrical theory during the workday. They also discussed the need for some kind of "human re-

Clara Fraser, Feminist Rebel

Born in 1923 and raised by radical immigrant Jewish trade unionists in Los Angeles, Clara Fraser arrived in Seattle in 1946 and never stopped organizing. She was initially an active member of the Socialist Workers Party (SWP). Blacklisted after participating in the Boeing strike of 1948 as an assembly-line electrician, she then held a variety of jobs, while hounded by the FBI, and worked in the SWP to support labor, anti-discrimination, and an end to the Vietnam War.

In the mid-1960s, Fraser helped found the FSP and RW and was key to formulating their socialist feminist platforms. She worked in various federally funded anti-poverty programs, first at the Seattle Opportunities and Industrialization Center, a job training school, then at an offshoot of the federal Model Cities program. During these years, she also raised two sons and divorced two husbands.

Freedom Socialist

In June 1973, Fraser was hired as a trainer at City Light and then assigned to coordinate the utility's incipient ETT program for women. Superintendent Gordon Vickery thought he was getting an experienced community organizer who would help the utility address its documented and illegal discrimination without rocking the boat. Instead Fraser took Vickery and City Light at their word, and created a program that would force the utility to train and hire women with the expectation they would progress to journey-level field work, at journey-level wages. She also organized and led utility workers in ultimately successful challenges to Superintendent Vickery's autocratic administrative support of blatant worksite discrimination and harassment.

Fraser speaking at the July 1974 Radical Women conference in Seattle.

Within a year of when Fraser started work at the utility, ten women had come on as ETTs and Fraser had been removed as the program's coordinator. She was laid off from City Light less than two years from when she was hired.

Fraser filed a complaint charging political and sex discrimination. It took nine years and a Superior Court appeal before she won damages and reinstatement at City Light, where she once again joined the fray of workplace organizing.

After retiring from the utility in 1986, Fraser continued to provide leadership in the FSP and RW, and to write for the *Freedom Socialist* newspaper. She died February 24, 1998.

lations training for foremen and supervisors" of ETTs.[30] "Human re-lations" was the term, at the time, for training employees, especially management, on how to meet worksite requirements and policies of affirmative action and Equal Employment Opportunity law.

Throughout September and October of 1973, there were lots of ETT Planning Committee meetings and lots of memos documenting them. Administrative considerations were analyzed, such as whether current city employees could apply to the program, how to legally make the ETT program exclusively for women, whether federal fund-ing from the Department of Labor could be used, and what related requirements might come with such funding.

At the same time the ETT committee was moving forward, the Seattle City Council passed the Seattle Fair Employment Practices Ordinance (Ordinance 102562), sponsored by Councilmember Jean-ette Williams. Members of the Freedom Socialist Party and Radical Women had successfully proposed the addition of "marital status," "sexual orientation" and "political ideology" to the list of non-discriminatory mandates. The ordinance increased pressure on City Light's new ETT program to successfully implement affirmative action.

City Councilwoman Jeanette Williams also had input on the ETT program itself. She agreed with an element brought forward by Clara Fraser that economic "disadvantage" should not be the main criteria for selecting the ETTs because many women were underemployed in traditional female jobs even if they were above the official poverty line. As Fraser stated in an October weekly activity report, Williams would support an ordinance change

> defining a broader concept of Affirmative Action so that we will
> not be bound by the ridiculously low income levels for minorities
> and women mandated by the Dept. of Labor for trainee projects.[31]

The DOL requirements and funding related to the ETT program would continue to be one of many contested elements even after the program was underway.

Several training components were also under discussion. What tasks would be included and how would the ETTs' performance on them be evaluated? How would the crew chiefs and supervisors be involved? What would comprise its human relations training? Joan Williams, the utility's EEO officer, put forward a plan that involved creating an in-house human relations council to do the training for all City Light employees.

During 1973, Mayor Wes Uhlman was running for re-election. Former City Council Chair Liem Tuai campaigned against him on a platform of fiscal conservatism, with the backing of traditional downtown business interests, and it was a close race. But on November 6, Uhlman was narrowly reelected, with a margin of only 5,266 votes out of nearly 189,000 ballots cast.

Plans for the ETT program continued to move forward. Beginning in November 1973, Charlie Silvernale, IBEW #77's business representative for City Light, was included in the planning meetings as discussion focused on how to recruit women for the program.

By the end of the month, a memo from Bill Rheubottom reported several advancements he and Clara Fraser had made, including meetings with various supervisors at the utility's South Service Center "to obtain a clearer understanding of work stations and skills needed by electricians, in preparation for the forthcoming electrical trades trainee program for women." Rheubottom also explained that the ETT Planning Committee was working with Seattle's Personnel Department "to clarify problems involved in the Civil Service testing procedures, advertising content of job announcement, training sites and related matters."[32] At the end of December, Rheubottom reported a major breakthrough:

> The Washington State Human Rights Commission has approved our proposal that this program be advertised for women only, and the city Civil Service commission will be given the go-ahead to start preparing public recruiting announcements after the first of the year [1974].[33]

On January 1, 1974, Wes Uhlman began his second term as mayor of Seattle. On that same day, Gordon Vickery enacted a City Light budget that included a new position, Administrative Services director, to which he appointed Carole Coe, only three years out of

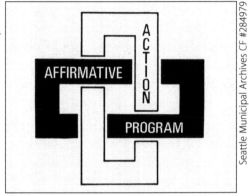

Cover detail from 1977 City Light quarterly report on hiring, retention, and training of people of color and women.

law school. Part of Coe's duties were to oversee the Training Division. On Coe's first day, Vickery had Rheubottom and Fraser give a presentation on the ETT program to his staff, including their new supervisor, Coe. This included an outline, a timeline, and program content.

In mid-January, Clara Fraser sent a memo to ETT project planners documenting two elements of the program:

> Formal schooling for the trainees [would] be on Company time.... Agreement that workday wouldn't be interrupted for classes....
>
> ...work up to 95% of helpers' pay. While the program lasts for two years, trainees will move according to their own progress....[34]

(Later decisions mandating *unpaid* class time and a much lower rate of pay would be part of the ETTs' eventual discrimination claim.)

Fraser also noted the estimated budget for the ETT program, $267,000, and the makeup of the new planning committee: herself, Charlie Silvernale (IBEW #77), Joan Williams (EEO officer), two foremen, a personnel supervisor, and Ken Hunich (City Light's director of Distribution).

About two weeks later, the utility allocated a significantly smaller amount for the ETT program, $210,000, which provided each trainee with $9,354 for the six months remaining in 1974. At the time, the federal Department of Labor was expected to reimburse City Light for the women's education costs, work clothes, and equipment. But payment for the latter two items never materialized, although Rheubottom continued to argue with a DOL representative about "observ[ing] federal…poverty ceilings" versus "help[ing] implement EEO and civil rights for women programs."[35] The DOL representative also thought there would be "a very good chance" that, come July, there could be federal funding for the ETT program.

Then came word: the city's all-powerful Office of Management and Budget had approved the ten slots for women.

Meanwhile, Clara Fraser had convinced IBEW #77 leadership that the ETTs should join the union within six months of being hired, as a separate bargaining unit. Rheubottom suggested this be affirmed during negotiations with the union.

On Valentine's Day, Rheubottom sent Coe another of his regular activity reports. The Training Division and the Civil Service Department had locked down final details of the interview and evaluation process for ETT applicants. Rheubottom closed his report noting applications would be accepted for three weeks, beginning that day.

WOMEN ONLY !
EQUAL EMPLOYMENT OPPORTUNITY

ELECTRICAL TRADES TRAINEE

THE CITY OF SEATTLE CIVIL SERVICE DEPARTMENT
200 MUNICIPAL BUILDING   FOURTH AND CHERRY STREETS
SEATTLE, WASHINGTON 98104   Telephone: 583-2682

ELECTRICAL TRADES TRAINEE

#25-74 - Non-Competitive

STARTING PAY: $3.5057 per hour, with merit increases to $4.4368 per hour.

WHO CAN APPLY: Women who meet the age and selection criteria.
Note: This is in compliance with the City of Seattle's Affirmative
Action Program to insure equal opportunity for women and has been
approved by the State of Washington Human Rights Commission.

AGE: Seattle women maximum age 62 years; However, the Lighting Department
advises that the maximum apprentice age is 34 and applicants must have
successfully completed the training program and qualified by civil
service exam by this age to be appointed to Line Crew Helper/Apprentice
Line Worker and Electrician-Constructor Apprentice.

SELECTION: The major objective of this program is to help occupationally
disadvantaged women to obtain regular City jobs with career advancement
opportunity. Those to be employed must be:

a. Culturally, socially or economically disadvantaged as a result of
exclusion from successful career employment with advancement
opportunity. The deficiency must be such that it can be overcome during a training period of up to two years. In addition,
they must meet one of the following requirements:

b. Be a member of a poor family, as defined by the U.S. Department of
Labor, OR

c. Be unemployed or underemployed.
Note: Women City of Seattle employees may qualify for this program
if they are low-skilled or unskilled, underemployed and presently
employed in positions that effectively preclude meaningful career
employment with advancement opportunities with the City.

EXAMINATION: The exam is an interview and evaluation of your background
and qualifications and may include a demonstration of your ability to
connect wires on a wiring board. It is essential that each applicant
submit an accurate and complete record of education and experience.

WHAT IS THE JOB: This is trainee level work performed under supervision
on equipment, machines, appliances, or systems; or on the construction
and maintenance of overhead electrical power distribution facilities,
including a variety of manual tasks on the ground and underground as a
temporary member of a team; or assisting in the operating of an electric power generating or distribution substation; and includes related
work as required. This is hard physical work; it involves carrying
equipment, working in bad weather and wearing heavy protective clothing.

WHAT IS THE FUTURE: This program provides an opportunity for training in
preparation for a position as an Electrician-Constructor Apprentice or
a Line Crew Helper/Apprentice Line Worker who earns $4.53 to $6.43 per
hour, or as an Electrical Helper who earns $4.67 to $5.07 per hour. A
satisfactory medical exam, given by the City, must be completed prior
to appointment. The program will include classes and on-the-job training. The program will continue for up to two years. It can end at any
time the employee is qualified for and accepted into regular City
employment.

NOTE: Residence within the Corporate City Limits of Seattle is required
for application and appointment.

NJJ:ja   MINORITY WOMEN ARE ACTIVELY ENCOURAGED TO APPLY.

Important: See reverse side for further information and instructions.

Official Bulletin Series 25-74   Filing closes MARCH 7, 1974.
              (2-14-74)
                                        ELECTRICAL TRADES TRAINEE

City Light flyer seeking women for the Electrical Trades Trainee program.

Breaking In

The ten women in City Light's 1974 ETT program were not the very first women in the electrical trades at City Light. Joanne Simmons seems to be the first, eventually advancing to hydro station operator on the Skagit project, a group of three dams on the Skagit River. But the ETTs *were* the first to enter a program designed to break down City Light's barriers to women in the electrical field crews, and the first to work on the Overhead (line), Underground, and Substation division crews, some of the most dangerous work in the U.S. (See summary of work divisions on page 127.)

Even the hiring process for the female ETT program was new territory. From the program's first conceptualization, the schedule was more than ambitious for outreach to possible applicants, applicant selection, and locking down the final program content. Applications were accepted from February 14 through March 7, 1974, although these three weeks were also when community outreach to broaden the applicant pool occurred. Clara Fraser used her connections with various feminist organizations to spread the word.

On February 21, City Light EEO Officer Joan Williams and a representative from either the city's Personnel or Civil Service department began reviewing applications.

But even while ETT applications were being accepted, Vickery and Coe began to undercut other elements of the Training Division. Vickery abruptly cancelled a shorthand class, developed by Fraser, because of "poor planning and lack of coordination."[36] In reality, it was because *men* had signed up for the course. The training was technically open to all Lighting Department employees, but Vickery had presumed only women would sign up for a course designed to upgrade the skills of low-paid clericals. Clara Fraser protested the cancellation, as did Rheubottom and two EEO officers.

There was also an ongoing fight over human relations training for management. Since February, Vickery and Coe had been restructuring this training, changing it from a stand-alone program into part of a larger management program, and moving it from the Training Division to the EEO Office. Then Vickery cancelled the slots that had been reserved for people of color and women. When Fraser protested, Coe and Vickery issued a "training moratorium."

Coe then wrote a memo blaming Fraser for mobilizing protests over this moratorium. Coe declared Vickery felt Fraser "had severe shortcomings." Coe further instructed Fraser's supervisor, Bill Rheubottom, to be "more critical" of her.[37]

Meanwhile, the ETT program was being finalized, including *its* human relations training for the foremen who would be working with the female trainees. After the dust-up over such training for management, this component of the ETT program was delayed for two months.

On March 7, concurrent with the closing date for applications, the first round of ETT applicant screening began. According to Clara Fraser's reports, more than 300 women had applied. After a first round of interviews with the city's Civil Service Department, 112 advanced as semi-finalists.

City Light then conducted its own applicant interviews, which brought the roster down to 56 by the beginning of April.

One of the ten women eventually hired as an ETT, Jody Olvera, had seen the job advertised on a flyer at an unemployment office. She remembered:

> The interview was partially about being tough enough to do the job, the work, face the attitudes on the worksites....
>
> I wanted a job that paid as well as this. I wanted a job that had the possibility of a future, that required skilled labor.[38]

Another ETT, Angel Arrasmith, remembers being asked why City Light should hire her:

> I told them I would be an asset. That I'd built a radio when I was 11 or 12, that I knew things about wiring from helping my dad install a radio into a car when I was 13. That I'd always been very mechanical, taking things apart to see, then I put it back together....

I told them what they wanted to hear, and made them know I could back it up.[39]

A number of Radical Women members applied, and four were among the top 20 selected for the final round of interviews. While sharing the desire to work in challenging, well-paid jobs in a traditionally male, unionized trade, they were also motivated by the goals expressed in a 1974 position statement adopted by the membership, *Radical Women in the House of Labor: An Historic Re-entry:*

> [This] has been a time of new stirrings in the sleeping house of labor among women and minority workers. It's an organism we are helping to shake into struggle by raising the demands of workers on the bottom and working with them to pressure union leaders to *lead.*[40]

While the applicants were being screened, basic elements of the training program were still under discussion. The city's Public Service Careers program was in the process of developing the so-called "training model," which seems to refer to the subject components of the program. Plans for the ETTs' orientation were also moving forward, including arrangements for a booklet on basic electrical theory. Rheubottom informed Coe that the ETT Planning Committee had once more unanimously recommended that the ETTs be allowed to join IBEW #77.

At the end of March, one of Rheubottom's activity reports described changes in the program that would fuel protests from Fraser and, once they were hired, most of the ETTs:

> 4. We feel badly about the decision to eliminate the clothing allowance for the trainees, since previous male trainees all received it....
>
> 5. Steve Ratliff...is working with us to develop a special drivers' training course for the trainees as the first activity on their on-the-job agenda.... [T]he course will involve about 3 days of intensive practice with every kind of truck and vehicle that the trainees will have to drive.[41]

The commitment to *intensive* training for driving City Light's big rigs was just one element of the program that would disappear once training began. No explanation was given for why the clothing allowance had been eliminated but it related in part to the lack of federal Department of Labor funding for the program.

The ETT committee, which included Fraser, recognized there were problems with the applicant pool: "Women applying with too much education [and] not enough minority women recruited."[42] When the DOL finally made it clear it would *not* fund the program, a representative of the committee tried to push back:

> a. Tried to convince DOL to suspend poverty guidelines for women ETTs so 7 out of 10 positions could be funded by DOL...
>
> b. DOL refused saying $2,000 is maximum earning so applicants can be considered disadvantaged
>
> c. DOL suggested PSC get funds from Manpower Consortium[43]

Rheubottom also informed the committee that any problems it had with the City Light administration's training model would fall on deaf ears, since

> the 9th floor [Vickery's office] recommended training model... [and] said the lack of such a model was why programs weren't successful in the past.[44]

April 1974 would turn out to be a very cruel month for Gordon Vickery. In mid-March, he had issued his own harsh and unilateral "Disciplinary Code" to all employees. On April 9, one supervisor applied it to two lineworker crew chiefs, Robert Whitlow and Arnold Schroeder, disciplining them for supposedly taking excessive coffee breaks. Walt Sickler, a former lineman, was manager of Overhead Construction at the time. In a much later interview, Sickler explained his part in this incident:

> There were directives regarding the conduct of the crews and such as that. There was one [directive] that when the crews completed a job they were to return to the shop and resupply their trucks and discontinue the practice of stopping somewhere to

kill time until time to go in. It was reported in the White Center area that there were two crews that were stopping regularly in the substation. I was the manager of those crews at the time so I investigated it. I talked to the foremen and, yes, they admitted they had been stopping there and they would drink coffee for 15 or 20 minutes before they came in. [This was a common way of taking mandatory breaks that had been skipped during the workday.]

I reported back to my immediate superior, Ken Hunich, who talked to the Assistant Superintendent Julian Whaley. The word was back from Mr. Whaley that they were to receive three days off. When Mr. Hunich reported that to me I indicated that if you require that, it's going to cause some real problems with the Line Division. Line crew foremen hadn't been disciplined before. And the word came back that they would receive the three days off. So I went down and told the two line crew foremen that they would receive three days off for misconduct. Their reaction was, "we don't have to put up with this." They walked out the door, got in their cars, and went down to the union hall.[45]

City Light's contract with IBEW #77 had expired ten days before this incident, and the local's members had just voted on the latest contract offer. Before the results of that vote were counted, about 700 union members walked out in a wildcat strike. (A wildcat strike is a spontaneous work stoppage not pre-authorized by the union.) On Wednesday, April 10, the Associated Press reported:

About 700 Seattle City Light electrical workers stayed off the job...in a dispute over potential disciplinary action against two men accused of "goofing off."

"They're all out as far as we know," City Light spokesman [sic] Joan Whiley said after the union workers failed to show up on the job as linemen, station operators, appliance servicemen and dispatchers.[46]

When interviewed, Vickery both back-pedaled and threatened the striking workers:

City Light Superintendent Gordon Vickery said the suspensions were only proposed by the men's supervisor and require Vickery's signature before the orders would go into effect. He said he did not sign the orders and is willing to negotiate the matter if workers go back on the job.

"It [the violation] involves quitting work early and goofing off," Vickery said.[47]

The next day, Clara Fraser received a call from Miles Chamberlain, a walkout leader, requesting she come to a meeting of the striking electrical workers to hear their grievances. Chamberlain also asked Fraser to bring a delegation from the City Light administration building.

Fraser and other office workers went to the meeting, agreed with the striking workers' cause, and were ready to support them. But first they wanted a commitment from IBEW #77 that it would work to bring City Light's mostly unorganized clerical staff into the local. (Known as industrial unionism, this model for union representation

First day of the City Light walkout. Workers flood Seattle City Council chambers to demand the firing of Superintendent Gordon Vickery.

was similar to what already existed at Puget Sound Power & Light, a private regional utility, and is different from craft union representation, which only covers workers in a particular trade.) An agreement was made that the local would work to get clericals into IBEW #77, although it is unclear to what degree the local's formal leadership was part of this commitment.

Within a day, the majority of City Light's clerical workers, led by Fraser and others, joined the walkout even as EEO Officer Joan Williams circulated around the building, telling people not to go out. One of Fraser's co-leaders on the walkout was Marilyn Bircher, a plain-speaking City Light accountant and single mother, who had worked her way up from being a personnel clerk. Bircher had started leading the city's clericals to unionize because at City Light "the lowest paid laborer was paid $50 more a month than the highest paid clerk."[48]

Estimates of some 1,000 City Light workers physically walked out, and stayed out, for 11 days. ETT-to-be Margie Wakenight, then working in the administration building, was one. On the same day clericals joined the wildcat strike, some 500 City Light workers marched to City Hall to protest Vickery's autocratic management style and his demeaning comments to the press about workers "goofing off."

The day after his co-workers walked out, Bill Rheubottom, who had stayed on the job, let Carole Coe know he'd sent out letters informing 56 ETT applicants they had made it to final interviews. Rheubottom also informed Coe that Fraser was participating in the walkout, although it is impossible to believe Coe wasn't already fully aware of this.

Strikers circulated a petition to oust Vickery, and gathered signatures. Vickery wanted to assign blame and held a meeting that included Coe and Rheubottom in which he blasted Rheubottom

> for not having done [a] good job in training division...stated that Clara seemed to be running Training Division...and complained that memos were being sent out from the division that weren't being approved by Coe first.[49]

(Coe's approval was not a requirement at the time.)

Once Fraser sided with the strikers, Vickery went after her. He and Coe instigated a red-baiting effort to discredit Fraser and the walkout, although Vickery had known Fraser was a socialist and feminist when he hired her. Her commitment to social justice and feminism as well as her history of successful community organizing were part of why he thought she could make the ETT program work. But as Marilyn Bircher recalled 25 years later:

> During the walkout, Clara started making her real self known. And City Light found out they hadn't hired a yes-man at all.[50]

Vickery also distributed sections of Fraser's supposedly confidential FBI file to management, while Coe announced that a friend in the FBI told her the walkout was "communist-inspired."[51]

In the meantime, those who had walked out realized they shared common problems. As Bircher described it:

> For the first time the employees at City Light...came together at one spot during that walkout and had a chance to talk to each other and we found out that our problems...were...common throughout the department.[52]

IBEW #77 leadership was experiencing its own nightmare in relation to its members' unauthorized walkout. But since the local had *not* called the strike, it couldn't declare it over. At the same time, the local's leaders were angry at Vickery's ongoing vilification of those who worked at City Light and at his disciplinary measures, because they violated protocols outlined in the union contract. And Local #77 *was* interested, at this point, in bringing City Light's clerical workers into the local.

But union officers could not do so without the approval of the IBEW International in Washington, D.C. Charlie Silvernale, who represented the local's City Light workers, later recalled that the International made it very clear to him and John Starcevich (the local's business manager): they needed to get their members back to work or the International would step in and "resolve" the matter. It was understood this meant the International would appoint its own local leadership, putting #77 into receivership. Silvernale had side

City Light accountant Marilyn Bircher helped mobilize office workers to join the walkout.

conversations with strike leaders and waited.

Megan Cornish, a member of Radical Women and soon to be an ETT, recalls that Fraser and other leaders of the building workers were presented with a *fait accompli:* the electrical workers were going back. The non-union militants, including office workers, had no vote on the matter, but they used their influence to help craft the conditions of the workers' return.

On the following Monday, April 15, Vickery, in the face of a 38,000-signature petition to oust him, pledged that there would be no reprisals for the walkout if everyone came back to work, and that he would reinstate the two suspended lineworkers. He agreed to establish a labor-management committee to negotiate a bill of rights and responsibilities that would replace his autocratic disciplinary code. Vickery also signed off on creation of another committee, the Public Review Committee, which was to investigate his administrative practices.

Vickery, Mayor Uhlman, three workers who had led the walkout, and three of City Light's supervisors, signed an agreement that Friday.

The walkout was finally brought to a close on April 20, 1974, with the following agreement:

1) An eleven-member citizens committee would conduct an open review of City Light, with particular attention to fiscal and administrative management, and report its findings to Mayor Uhlman by September 15, 1974.

2) The proposed suspensions of Robert Whitlow and Arnold Schroeder would be reviewed by a three-person committee chaired by the Dean of the University of Washington Law School.

3) The March 21, 1974, disciplinary policy would be removed and a City Light employee's Bill of Rights and Responsibilities would be developed by a committee of three representatives chosen by the employees and three appointed by Vickery.

4) No reprisals, actual or implied, would be instituted against any city employees involved in the walkout.

5) The petitions requesting Vickery's removal as superintendent would be kept on file.

6) The proposed probationary period against Whitlow and Schroeder would be removed.[53]

The walkout had ended, but bad feelings did not.

At the end of April, Vickery adopted and circulated a multi-page memo formalizing new City Light policies and procedures, incorporating Seattle's Fair Employment Practices Ordinance (Ordinance 102562, adopted some seven months earlier).

The Bill of Rights and Responsibilities Committee (BRRC) held its first meeting on April 21. Clara Fraser was elected as one of three employee representatives and also the employees' co-chair of the committee. (The other co-chair was appointed by management.) Marilyn Bircher was asked by members of both this committee and the Public Review Committee to coordinate their intersecting work and dispense information between the two groups. She was also part of a working committee that helped prepare people who wanted to bring grievances before the Public Review Committee.

Vickery, meanwhile, in a transparent attack on Fraser, requested that all City Light directors and their staff "evaluate" the Training Division and send these evaluations to his office.

At the beginning of May, Carole Coe sent a memo to Assistant Superintendent Julian Whaley stating the Training Division was "not following thru with work assigned...What they do is very poor."[54] She then received a memo from Joe Recchi of the City Light Engineering Division asserting the Training Division was "Not providing necessary services for his division.... Work is hit and miss."[55] (Recchi would become the utility's assistant superintendent within a year.)

Over the course of several days, other division directors sent memos to Coe outlining their criticisms of the Training Division. None were very specific, stating only "Training Division of little value" or it "lacks overall management." At best, one respondent "appreciated brochures Training Division has sent out."[56]

City employees and others who had supported the walkout continued their offensive, focusing on Mayor Wes Uhlman, who had backed Vickery's handling of the walkout. A recall petition against Uhlman was filed May 6, but less than two weeks later, Seattle's legal counsel rejected the petition as legally invalid.

With everyone back at work, the ETT program moved forward. The ETT Planning Committee again met and again discussed the program's human relations, driver training, and physical conditioning components. No decisions were reported in Rheubottom's summary memo to Coe.

By mid-May, interviews with the top 53 applicants had been scheduled for late May and early June. Interviews would be conducted by an "Interviewing panel...comprised of five people, representing overhead, underground, station construction, training, EEO office, with alternates available from personnel."[57] Final selection would be complete by June 6, with ETT orientation scheduled to begin June 24.

Clara Fraser kept working hard on the program. She sent the ETT committee a summary of program elements and a first draft of an ETT program "Fact Sheet,"

> the product of several months of discussion by all members of the Trainee Committee, which had full responsibility for planning and implementing the ETT program. The factsheet was used as the basis for discussion at the crew chief orientation.[58]

The fact sheet described all aspects of the ETT program, including "objectives, purpose, responsibilities, program design and schedule, salary, promotions, union membership, toilet facilities, on-the-job and classroom training, and progress reports."[59]

Carole Coe immediately responded with memos stating the entire program was to have started in mid-April (when the walkout had been in full swing) and that she wanted to be "advise[d] why the program has been so long delayed."[60]

At the time of Coe's memo, the ETT hiring process was not even complete, and there is no documentation that the training program had ever been scheduled to start in April. Nonetheless, Clara Fraser came back the next day with a revised schedule for the development of the entire program. Rheubottom took two weeks to send a written response to Coe's memo, outlining a number of "unforeseen delays" and also making clear that the federal Department of Labor had never actually committed to funding for the ETT program.

By the beginning of June 1974, the final ETT interviews had been conducted. At least one of the field representatives on the ETT committee had signed off on Fraser's program plans. Fraser was firming up the physical conditioning component. This was to include a swimming program with the city's Parks Department that a Public Service Careers representative had initiated. (Fraser had consulted with physical training experts who told her swimming would be the quickest way to build overall strength.)

On June 6, 1974, ten women were selected for the trainee program by the five-person hiring panel, which included Fraser. Bill Rheubottom sent an activity report to Coe noting:

> The interviewing is completed, after 5 solid days of work,
> and the selections were made after six hours of discussion and

MEETING
OF
CITY LIGHT EMPLOYEES
TUES, MAY 28
7:00 PM
SNOQUALMIE ROOM
SEATTLE CENTER

ATTEND AND DO YOUR PART IN OUR CONTINUING STRUGGLE FOR EMPLOYEE RIGHTS AND EFFECTIVE MANAGEMENT

DISCUSSION OF OUR FINANCIAL AND ORGANIZATIONAL SITUATIONS

REPORTS FROM:
  WHITLOW-SCHROEDER REVIEW COMMITTEE
  MANAGEMENT REVIEW COMMITTEE
  BILL OF RIGHTS AND RESPONSIBILITIES COMMITTEE
  RECALL COMMITTEE

evaluation by the 5-person interviewing panel consisting of Joan Williams, Ray Naud (Station Construction), Larry Christenson (Overhead), Don Moore (underground) and Clara Fraser.

...a 5-person panel is an unusually large one, making decisions based on consensus especially difficult....

The panel feels it has selected top notch people; now it is up to us to hold them....

We are meeting with PSC [Public Service Careers] to finalize Trainee Orientation plans, and the following two weeks of Pre-Placement Training.[61]

The next morning, a false and inflammatory leaflet was widely circulated at the utility. Someone at City Light wanted Fraser out, and wanted to discredit her as an assertive and respected co-chair of the Bill of Rights and Responsibilities Committee. Circumstantial evidence pointed to Carole Coe as author of the flyer, because once again someone in City Light was red-baiting Fraser for her political history as a socialist, feminist, and community organizer:

A sloppily drawn, libelous flyer, purporting to advertise a June 8 speech by Fraser entitled "Organizing to Oust Uhlman and Vickery," was anonymously mailed to the homes of about fifteen walkout leaders. The flyer also mysteriously appeared on bulletin boards, walls and in large stacks in City Light buildings and facilities all over town....

The source of the flyer was never uncovered, nor was it ever determined how hundreds of copies got past Carole Coe's tight building security to appear simultaneously first thing in the morning at most City Light work locations.[62]

Even Eldon Crothers, a member of the Executive Board of the Civil Service League in Seattle, was mailed a copy.

The flyer claimed "Trotskyite Communist" Fraser would be speaking at Freeway Hall (headquarters of the Freedom Socialist Party and Radical Women). It "revealed" Fraser had voted for socialist electoral candidates in the past.

Some of the leaders and supporters of the recent walkout were confused, angry, and suspicious about where the leaflet had come from; other City Light workers wanted to know if Fraser and other walkout spokespeople really were communists. Most thought the flyer was a fake. Bob Leighton and Art Myers, who had been leaders of the Uhlman recall attempt, went to Freeway Hall the night of the purported meeting to see if anything *was* going on.

> When no one showed up, they concluded that the whole incident was an underhanded smear campaign attempting to get walkout leaders to think that Fraser wasn't the kind of person they wanted to be involved with. As far as Leighton [Recall Committee chair] was concerned, it didn't do that.[63]

Within a week, Bill Rheubottom sent a memo to Coe asking for a meeting to discuss the flyer, but there is no indication such a meeting was ever held.

A few weeks later, Fraser attended one of the ongoing employee mass meetings to answer questions and doubts from co-workers about the hoax flyer. Fraser called the leaflet a flagrant divide-and-conquer tactic by management, then described her political philosophy of advocating for *all* workers to unify around common grievances. She also offered to resign from the Bill of Rights and Responsibilities Committee, if that's what her co-workers wanted. They instead applauded, and asked her to stay on.

The clock kept ticking. With the ETT program scheduled to begin in less than two weeks, human relations training for crew chiefs and field supervisors still hadn't been locked down.

The Friday before the trainees were to begin work, Clara Fraser sent the ETT committee's pre-placement schedule to Coe, outlining its content, including a class on electrical theory. The pre-placement part of the program was slated to run from June 24 through July 8. In her memo, Fraser notified Coe that Ken Hunich, director of the Distribution Division, had approved both the schedule and the participation of members of his division.

But Overhead Supervisor Earl Willey wasn't happy about what the committee had come up with. He sent his own memo directly to Vickery challenging elements of the pre-placement plan:

I do not believe that the orientation for a new employee need require more than one day....

Much of this program smacks of personal, political, and social ideology and I do not believe the interest of City Light is well served by being a forum for such.[64]

The following Monday, June 24, 1974, ten women showed up for their first day as Electrical Trades Trainees.

Megan Cornish in lineworker school, 1976.

Affirmative Action Warriors

On Monday, June 24, 1974, ten women began work at Seattle City Light in the first program of its kind in the U.S.: Angel Arrasmith, Teri Bach, Megan Cornish, Heidi Durham, Jennifer Gordon, Daisy Jones, Letha Neal, Jody Olvera, Margie Wakenight, and Patty Wong.

Selected through an intense, multi-stage process, the ETTs included two Black women, a Chicana, and an Asian American. Olvera, Gordon, Bach, Cornish and Durham (at 21, the youngest) were all active in Seattle's feminist movement. The latter three were members of Radical Women and the Freedom Socialist Party. Margie Wakenight was a clerk for the supervisor of substation engineering, and worked in the City Light office building. Bach, Jones and Wakenight were single mothers. Several ETTs were fairly open as lesbians.

Marilyn Bircher, one of the Pied Pipers for building workers during the walkout, later commended Fraser's role in the hiring process (and Fraser's opinion certainly carried weight as designer of the program, though she was only one of five interviewers):

> In the process of selecting the women who were going to be in the program, she was very careful...she selected the ten toughest that she could find. The ten toughest, the ten smartest, and the ten she felt would really stick with it.[65]

The women's reasons for taking on this grueling, dangerous work in a potentially confrontational atmosphere included: earning higher pay, being able to support children as a single parent, wanting to show women could do the job, and the opportunity to develop their technical skills and interests. In 1975, Heidi Durham also expressed what fueled the three socialist feminist participants:

> We felt a deep responsibility to be examples of principled

working-class militancy, to expose the class warfare that hides behind "labor-management relations," and to show that the way to win against the employer is through the class solidarity forged when privileged, white-male workers understand that they must support the demands of the lower-paid and lower-skilled workers, predominantly women and minorities, in their midst, in return for concerted action by the total workforce.[66]

At the start of their first day of work, the ETTs were ushered into Superintendent Vickery's office for a press conference he had previously arranged. While smiling and posing for pictures with the new hires, Vickery talked up the ETTs' future at City Light. Megan Cornish and others cannot forget Vickery telling them that any one of them could become superintendent of City Light; happy to imply the women were destined to have careers at the utility. (He would later vehemently reject this notion.)

With that, the ETT program was underway. The first week's training was a general orientation to the utility. The ETTs attended

informational presentations on city and City Light organization, rules and policies; employee benefits and evaluations; and tours of City Light substations and other major operations facilities.[67]

At the end of this week, three of the women (Gordon, Olvera, and Wong) met with EEO Officer Joan Williams to complain the program "was boring," and to explain they wanted more hands-on, craft-related instruction. This is what the second and third weeks of the pre-placement program had been designed to do. However, the exact content and training components of the second week were a moving target even after the ETTs started.

As ETT coordinator, Clara Fraser was in the thick of the conflict over what should constitute pre-placement training as well as other elements of the larger program. For example, even before the program started, Carole Coe had done her best to minimize any human relations training if it was recommended by Fraser, despite the fact that the design and implementation of this aspect of training was a significant part of Clara Fraser's job.

Press conference on ETTs' first day. Left to right: hydro station operator Joanne Simmons, ETT Daisy Jones, ETT coordinator Clara Fraser, EEO Officer Joan Williams, City Light Superintendent Vickery, ETT Teri Bach.

During the program's first week, the Public Review Committee was also holding hearings on the work climate at City Light. (This committee, part of the April 1974 walkout settlement, was tasked with investigating Vickery's administrative practices.) On the first day of the ETT program, Fraser gave testimony to the committee, documenting the roadblocks she had encountered when she tried to set up human relations trainings at City Light. She also spoke about the administration's contempt for its employees, and how it refused to provide training that would allow City Light workers to upgrade their skills. She described "top management's" contradictory policies on affirmative action, training, and safety, and concluded that the administration was "willful…arbitrary…capricious…erratic…closed-in…suspicious and…far less than candid."[68]

The next night, Carole Coe gave testimony, and did her best to rebut everything Fraser had said.

At the end of the first week of the ETT program, on the same day three ETTs had gone to the EEO officer to complain, Fraser sent memos to various field supervisors to confirm the dates and times of pre-placement training, set to begin the following Monday.

Instead, management decided the two weeks of hands-on and classroom training would be cut in half. Gordon Vickery, Carole Coe, and Walt Sickler (supervisor of Overhead Construction) peremptorily reduced the ETTs' pre-placement training to one week. Later that day, July 3, the women received word their training was curtailed. They immediately called ETT coordinator Clara Fraser. Then they tried to meet with Vickery. Megan Cornish recalled:

> When our program was cancelled, the training part, it was [Daisy Jones] who was our leader. She immediately called up Vickery's office and in her sexiest voice said, "Is Gordon there?" Trying to find out if we'd be able to storm his office. Because he was known as a womanizer and she knew that was our best shot for getting that information....[69]

Fraser reported on these events to the Public Review Committee just one month later:

> I was attending a meeting of the Bill of Rights and Responsibilities Committee at SSC [City Light's South Service Center], and received a distress call from all the trainees at NSC [North Service Center], informing me that the 2nd week of pre-placement [training] was cancelled! I couldn't believe it; I had not been consulted; I didn't know why and they didn't know why. They said they would leave for the [downtown administration] building immediately and meet me there, so we could find out what was happening. I called my supervisor—he claimed he didn't know what had happened.
>
> The trainees went to look for Ms. Coe and I came to my office, about 5 p.m.
>
> The next day was a holiday [4th of July]; nobody was in the building, nor would most directors be there on Friday. I couldn't find the trainees—they were with Ms. Coe—and I went looking for Mr. Vickery. Not in. I found Mr. Whaley [Assistant Superintendent Julian Whaley], who told me that at YESTERDAY'S staff meeting the "directors" objected to the physical conditioning, which in-

cluded swimming exercises..., to the driver's training, and to the electrical theory. No week was needed for such subjects, they said, and the trainees would report to work on [the following] Monday... on the job. Mr. Vickery and Ms. Coe agreed with the "directors." I asked him to convey my displeasure and disagreement to Mr. Vickery, and he said he would.

The trainees were very angry after talking to Coe, who said that swimming wasn't needed, nor theory, nor driving training—and who also accused me of "mis-managing" the program, organizing it secretly, and sundry other crimes. They wanted to talk to Vickery: I informed them he had said his door was always open, and he might see them on such a serious grievance. We agreed to all report to the [administration] building on Friday [July 5] to try to iron this out. I, as their supervisor, gave them permission to do this.[70]

That Friday, the ETTs met with Bill Rheubottom, Joan Williams, an instructor for in-service trainings, a representative of the Public Service Careers program, and Jack Driscoll (head of the city Personnel and Civil Service departments) to see if the pre-placement program could be saved.

Instead the ETTs were informed they would be docked two hours pay for meeting with Coe when they could not see Vickery. Clara Fraser challenged this, to no avail, at a staff meeting, explaining the ETTs' attempt to talk directly with Vickery had been authorized by both herself and Rheubottom. Fraser also formally requested clarification of the ETT job description. If the ETTs were in fact helpers, or doing work equivalent to a helper position, then they were doing it for a dollar an hour less than helpers. (There was no response at the time to Fraser's requests.)

Over the following weekend, ETT Patty Wong sent an incendiary letter to management outlining her disagreements with Clara Fraser and the rest of the ETTs. Wong's letter presented the same points she would give as testimony to the Public Review Committee the following week:

> One upsetting aspect of the Electrical Trades Trainee Program is the constant overemphasis being placed on the necessity of the

The ETTs

Angel Arrasmith
Renowned for her retort: "I'm more of a woman than you'll ever get and more of a man than you'll ever be!"

Teri Bach
Single mother, involved with union organizing at University of Washington, Radical Women member.

Megan Cornish
Literature major working at an industrial laundry, shared collective household with Clara Fraser.

Heidi Durham
The youngest at 21 years of age, former waitress, member of Radical Women and Freedom Socialist Party.

Jennifer Gordon
Office worker, active in Gay Liberation Front, women's health issues, and anti-war movement.

trainees establishing an intimate solidarity together—a tightly knit cadre, a sisterhood.... Then there are others who believe that part of their job consists of educating the entire male population of City Light on the equality, and perhaps, the superiority of the female sex in the electrical trades....

My strongest objection to this program, however, arises from my own bitter resentment to being utilized by Ms. Clara Fraser as a pawn in her political plays against City Light's "management" in the person of Mr. Gordon Vickery. It seems rather peculiar, to my way of thinking, how three of Clara Fraser's Radical Women managed to join the program.... [and] that Clara Fraser would encourage the suppression of divergent views critical of the program while...encouraging every move of the trainees that was critical of management....

I am tired of being pressured to become one with the group. I resent being told that my differing views jeopardize the success of the entire program. And I will not be used by Clara Fraser or any other political jockey in their mad drive for power.[71]

Vickery had also had enough of Fraser. On Tuesday, July 9, he removed her as ETT coordinator after she questioned Rheubottom on what was going on with changes in the program. At the end of an electrical theory class that Tuesday, the ETTs' pre-placement training was formally cancelled. They were told they were to report on the next morning for fieldwork assignments.

The ETTs objected in part because they had not yet received a paycheck, which several needed to buy expensive work clothes. (Federal Department of Labor funding for work clothing had never come through, nor had a City Light clothing allowance, although communication about both had been contradictory.)

The next morning, all ten women were sent into the field without equipment, work clothing, or most of the training that had been scheduled as part of their pre-placement program. If they had any questions or complaints, they could take them to the new ETT coordinator, Bill Rheubottom.

When asked about her first day, Megan Cornish had vivid memories. Prior to starting at City Light, she had been working at an industrial laundry for about a dollar an hour less than what she would make as an ETT, even at sub-helper wages. "Going into the program, it was really exciting...we were making history," she recalled. Nevertheless, Cornish had some rocky moments on her first day. She still ruefully remembers how she let slip her association with the "notorious" Clara Fraser—and how fast word travelled before she even got to her crew:

The ETTs

Daisy Jones
Worked with Model Cities in Los Angeles. Mother of five, the oldest ETT, a strong leader.

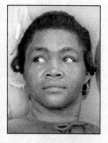

Letha Neal
Sure she could do the job because she'd "tinkered with electricity at home." Nicknamed "Cannonball" by crews.

Jody Olvera
Chicana lesbian separatist, active in the Seattle women's movement.

Margie Wakenight
Former office worker at Seattle City Light and single mother.

Patty Wong
Self-identified loner, the only ETT not to file discrimination charges against City Light.

Also see ETT Close-ups, page 184.

A couple of guys waylaid me on the way into the South Service Center to say "We hear *you* are a Radical Woman! Are *you* a Radical Woman?" And I had to go—gulp—"Well, yeah."[72]

When she got to her work crew:

I have never been strong and I've never been that mechanically oriented. I graduated in English literature from Cornell for god's sake. So I'm trying to do the thing, and my first day on the crew one of the guys says, "Well I'm willing to give you girls a chance, but I don't think you can do the job. And I think you should prove it to me whether you can do the job or not. You're supposed to be doing the helper job, and one of the things helpers have to do is haul a feeder arm" (which is particularly big and heavy; I think it was about six or eight feet long) "up the pole to the lineman." So luckily I had enough sense to know I may not be strong but I got a pretty good size pair of hips, and if I lean into the rope I should be able to pull the thing up.

For whatever reason, I managed to do that and I got it up the pole. And...that went around the crews. It definitely went around all of the South and North Line that I'd pulled a feeder arm up the pole.[73]

Each ETT was the only woman on her crew. They were paired up by workplace, with two ETTs at South Line, two at Network Underground, etc., the same two women staying together as they rotated through different job areas. So, for example, Cornish and Olvera worked out of the same locations, although they did not necessarily even see each other during the day.

Out with their crews, the women found many of the Black men, some of whom had been hired only a year or two earlier, to be their closest, and often, their *only* allies.

John Harris, who started at City Light in 1973, was one of only two African American apprentices at the time, and the other man soon quit. So he felt very alone. In remembering what it was like for the women, he said:

If you only knew how hard it was.... Letha [Neal] and I, when we met, we said, "There's two of us!"

I can only say it's been a joy for me working with the women at City Light, and you don't really know how hard it was. People'd play games all the time. They'd tell you to go get a hammer, but they'd hide all the hammers. Then you'd come back and they'd say, "Where's the hammer?" and they'd make you look like you didn't know what a hammer was.

Those were the itty-bitty things we had to overcome. But working together and being there together we kind of helped each other out....

Teri and Heidi and Megan...Margie...Jody, we came through the struggle together.[74]

During this period, IBEW #77 was not involved in any discussions about the ever-changing ETT program, although the trainees comprised their own bargaining unit within the local. Jody Olvera wrote about her experience that summer in a local feminist newsletter, *From the Ground Up:*

We kept hearing "You ten are in a fishbowl".... Everybody we deal with seems to have a different game going and different motivations and expectations of us....

The new union contract barely mentions our existence, and doesn't set down any ground rules or things like job definition, seniority, pay scale, or advancement possibilities and methods.[75]

Olvera denounced expectations others were making upon all of the ETTs:

We are expected to: pave the way for millions of other women, act as a united Musketeer-type team, be ten individually-successful Superwomen, develop "credibility" for women as real workers, educate the men (pretty tenderly and lovingly, it seems to some of us), and "be nice" to the men and not be "uptight, sullen, bitter, and brisk." Strangely enough, some of us hired on expecting just a job. We were quite aware of the unusual circumstances and lack of precedents, but we didn't know about the "humanitarian mission" aspect. We learned fast.[76]

There was another evening Public Review Committee meeting during the ETTs' first week out in the field. Six of the ETTs and Fraser presented their objections to the changes in the program and Fraser's removal as its coordinator. Patty Wong spoke against them, repeating the points she had made a week earlier in her letter to Vickery.

As she listened to Wong, Angel Arrasmith became so irate she "flew up out of [her] seat" and was "ready to paste her one right in the lip." [77] She was held back by the other trainees.

When the *Seattle Times* asked Vickery about the changes, he denied he had cancelled orientation or that he had ordered Fraser off the ETT program, saying "programs had been rescheduled and improved.... because field supervisors expressed concern with the content." [78] There is no documentation of such concerns.

A group of City Light workers sent their own memo to the Public Review Committee, charging that Vickery's "constant harassment and punitive measures designed to demoralize and intimidate involved employees" were a violation of the walkout agreement. They listed four incidents of reprisals, including Vickery's elimination of half the ETTs' pre-placement training and the fact Fraser had been "relieved of her assignment as [ETT] coordinator...because she exerted 'a negative influence' on the trainees and 'organized' them against Gordon Vickery." [79]

Now that Fraser was off the ETT program, City Light's administration focused on removing her from any other human relations training. Jack Driscoll (head of Seattle's Personnel and Civil Service departments) sent Vickery a memo suggesting that "all Human Relations Training be handled thru Human Rights Dept. so there won't be duplication of effort." [80]

Within a week, Vickery disbanded the Human Relations Council, comprised of Clara Fraser and other like-minded City Light workers. EEO Officer Joan Williams announced Vickery's decision at the group's last meeting, after telling those present the council was being used as "a political football." [81] Carole Coe immediately sent a memo to all the utility's division directors confirming Vickery's action.

In the meantime, Rheubottom notified the ETTs that the human relations training component of their program had been greatly reduced, while Coe informed Rheubottom that there would be a total of three two-hour sessions on human relations for City Light supervisors, with a longer seminar scheduled for August.

Carole Coe's July avalanche of memos to Vickery ended with her objection to Clara Fraser's "excessive" time involvement with the Bill of Rights and Responsibilities Committee.[82] This committee was mandated by the walkout settlement, and Fraser had been elected as its co-chair by the other workers on the committee, with the utility granting committee members work time to participate.

Fraser and the majority of the ETTs had had enough. The following Monday, August 5, 1974, they filed two separate discrimination complaints with Seattle's Office of Women's Rights and the Human Rights Department.

As of 2016, utility electrical work is still among the ten most dangerous jobs in the United States.

Powering Forward

Less than two months after they had started work, six of the ten ETTs collectively filed a sex discrimination complaint against Seattle City Light. Citing blatant on-the-job sex discrimination and harassment, Angel Arrasmith, Teri Bach, Megan Cornish, Heidi Durham, Daisy Jones, and Margie Wakenight filed complaint AO-165 with Seattle's Office of Women's Rights and Human Rights Department under the city's Fair Employment Practices Ordinance. This ordinance had been adopted and then amended during the two years before the ETT program began, as part of Seattle's movement toward affirmative action.

The ETTs' August 5 filing claimed

> unfair employment practices with respect to "terms and conditions" because of "sex"...based on the following facts....
>
> On June 24, 1974 we were employed by City Light as Electrical Trades Trainees. Our scheduled pre-placement training was immediately curtailed and rearranged. Shortly thereafter we were docked pay for attempting to discuss the matter with Superintendent Gordon Vickery. We believe we have been discriminated against on the basis of our sex.[83]

Three of the ETTs—Letha Neal, Jennifer Gordon, and Jody Olvera—were not signatories to the initial claim but signed on within months. Only Patty Wong never in any way supported the other trainees' challenges to implementation of the ETT program, nor their charges of discrimination and harassment.

Clara Fraser filed her own complaint at the same time the ETTs filed theirs, claiming discrimination on the basis of both sex and political ideology.

On the same day the complaints were filed, Daisy Jones, Angel Arrasmith, Margie Wakenight, Clara Fraser, and possibly other ETTs, gave testimony at another Public Review Committee meeting. Fraser

kept a copy of her comments, which, with dripping sarcasm, identified "exactly what Superintendent Vickery did to insure the 'success'
of [the ETT] program."[84]

Fraser started by describing the 1973 proposal from Public
Service Careers Director Richard Burt, "implementing the women
trainee project,"[85] as well as the original goals and work plan for the
ETT program. She also outlined significant difficulties the women
had faced from the day they were hired, as well as the administrative
directives and changes that led to her own abrupt removal as ETT
coordinator exactly one month earlier.

Fraser concluded her remarks by describing the discrimination
claims she and the six ETTs had filed that day:

> I, together with six of the trainees, have filed a charge against
> Gordon Vickery and City Light top management with the Depart-
> ment of Human Rights and the Office of Women's Rights.
> We charge Mr. Vickery with sex discrimination, with discrimina-
> tion on the basis of political ideology, and with illegal *reprisals.*[86]

She then introduced three of the ETTs, who gave their own
testimony: Daisy Jones, Angel Arrasmith, and Margie Wakenight.
When they finished, Fraser ended her testimony by encouraging the
committee to do more than report on what had already happened.

> You, the Public Review Committee, have an awesome respon-
> sibility. You are not "consultants" to management, to help them
> solve their problems, if they'd listen; you are instead a public,
> INVESTIGATORY BODY, like a Grand Jury, not a research team,
> and you must, in effect, determine whether or not an indictment
> is indicated.
> And, considering the evidence, it seems to me that you must
> bring in a verdict that the Vickery regime is indeed inept and irre-
> sponsible.[87]

Fraser and the ETTs who had filed the complaint weren't the
only ones testifying at this highly charged public meeting. ETT Patty
Wong defended and supported the reshaped and shortened ETT
program, once more making it clear she had no affinity for the other

ETTs or Clara Fraser. Further, Wong questioned why three members of Radical Women had made it into the ETT program, implying favoritism by Fraser despite the utility's intensive selection process. Wong stopped short of challenging Bach's, Cornish's, and Durham's qualifications as ETTs, instead implying their leftist politics tainted the entire program.

In addition that night, Doug Clifford, who had investigated employee grievances for presentation to the committee, testified Vickery was "secretive and dictatorial" and cited Vickery's "questionable priorities" relating to funding the remodel of a City Light auditorium.[88]

"Women Trainees Not Happy with Vickery," ran the next day's headline in the *Seattle Times*. The reporter summarized the previous evening's testimony, "Supt. Gordon Vickery is attempting to scuttle the program to train women,"[89] then described the discrimination claims filed by the ETTs and Fraser.

On the same day this article came out, Bill Rheubottom, Fraser's supervisor and her replacement as ETT coordinator, sent a memo to his boss, Carole Coe. In it, he reported that he and a representative from Public Service Careers had made an onsite visit to the ETTs' field supervisors a week before.

> Supervisors [are] satisfied with job conduct and performance of ETTs. Impressed with [ETTs'] eagerness to learn, functioning well....[90]

The Public Review Committee met again later that week. This time, EEO Officer Joan Williams and another woman spoke, rebutting Fraser, though their specific comments are not in available records.

The Public Review Committee finished its hearings, drafted its findings, and presented its report to Mayor Uhlman on August 20. The Bill of Rights and Responsibilities Committee, also part of City Light's walkout settlement, had already completed its draft "Bill of Rights and Responsibilities," and submitted it to the negotiators from both sides who had settled the walkout.

The document listed 14 employee rights, including respectful treatment and Constitutional guarantees, seven employee responsibilities, and 18 management responsibilities. Employee rights included: "clear, fair and visible standards and rules;...uniform application of standards,...equal opportunity and treatment, free from prejudicial, discriminatory or capricious action....courtesy, respect and consideration by all Department personnel....a safe and sanitary working environment....the right to competent management."[91]

While the Public Review Committee and the Bill of Rights and Responsibilities Committee were finishing their work, the ETTs were being interviewed by a City Light staffer about their program. Not surprisingly, the majority of the ETTs said they wanted Clara Fraser back as program coordinator, as well as reinstatement of the original program. The ETTs' comments were duly noted without further action.

Management hostility to the ETT program was reflected in work-site incidents. Megan Cornish remembered one example of crude racism targeting Black trainee Letha Neal:

> Somebody was walking down the [loading] dock and had a roll
> of black electrical tape in their back pocket and it fell out.... One of
> the guys said, "Oh, Letha, your asshole just fell out!"[92]

Each of the ETTs had her own way of dealing with such incidents. Cornish recalled how Daisy Jones, the other Black ETT, responded to racist harassment from her crew:

> Daisy locked the crew in the crew cab! Locked the doors on
> them from the outside and said, "You know you're not coming out
> until you learn a lesson about respect. And you're not going to give
> me any more shit. Ever."[93]

Angel Arrasmith, an unabashed, out-front "butch" lesbian, was notorious for her put-down to a hostile crew member:

> I'm more of a woman than you'll ever get and more of a man
> than you'll ever be.[94]

Jennifer Gordon remembered working on a line crew out of the South Service Center. After lunch break, someone on her crew sent her across the yard to get something. When she came back, her en-

Daisy Jones on City Light work crew, 1974.

tire crew was gone, without her. She went to the dispatcher.

> I told him my crew inadvertently left without me. The dispatch-
> er responded, "What makes you think it was inadvertent?" We
> both laughed, then he called the crew to come back, and they did.[95]

Margie Wakenight ignored harassment from her crews, most of the time, then found her own ways to deal with it. When she got into a crew cab plastered with female porn, she posted a picture of a nude, well-hung guy, which stayed up in the truck long after she was gone.

> If a guy mouthed off to me about taking a job away from a man
> trying to support a family, I'd tell him I have a family to feed too.
> This shut them up.[96]

The ETTs' discrimination case continued to move forward. Vickery sent the investigator for the Office of Women's Rights (OWR) a letter acknowledging the first meeting on the complaint would be to discuss specific discrimination charges. But the ETTs had filed their claim to accomplish more than simple enforcement of non-discrimination. As Heidi Durham wrote in a report to the 1975 conference of Radical Women, the ETTs to different degrees hoped

> to try to protect ourselves from being fired and to publicize and expose the underlying social issue of prejudice against us. Our claim also made clear our connection with the militant female leadership of the walkout [Clara Fraser and others] and their principle of workers' solidarity.[97]

Such feminist-worker solidarity caused many in the feminist community and progressive unionists to help the ETTs prepare and present their legal case. Without legal representation when they filed, the ETTs always had a strong legal defense team that included political strategists, volunteer attorneys, and, eventually, lawyers from the Office of Women's Rights. Radical Women and the Freedom Socialist Party had avidly followed and participated in the development of the ETT program, the walkout, and the recall campaign. Helping their sisters win the fight to integrate the field and keep their jobs was an organizing priority for both groups. Durham would later write:

> The Radical Women members [Durham, Cornish, and Bach] did most of the work to write the complaints and press releases organizing support in the community at large with Clara's help every step of the way.[98]

Radical Women felt it was vital to "encourage strong trainee solidarity in a unified front against management" in order to "demonstrate our unity to the union and demand fair representation by them."[99] Though others may not have shared this strategy, all except Patty Wong participated to some degree in coordinated self-defense activities such as press conferences, hearings, and signing group letters.

Putting in long hours after their grueling workdays, Durham, Cornish, and Bach pieced together an incredible paper trail documenting sex discrimination against the ETTs, as defined in the Seattle Fair Employment Practices Ordinance:

with respect to hiring, tenure, promotion, terms, conditions, wages or privileges of employment, or with respect to any matter directly or indirectly related to employment.[100]

Lawyer Eugene Moen began formally representing the Office of Women's Rights and the ETTs sometime in the fall of 1974, as the agency stepped up its investigation of the complaint. OWR investigator Barbara Carter and Joel Salmi, investigating Fraser's case for the Human Rights Department, also dedicated huge personal energy and time to the cases.

In addition to preparing their two cases and going to work every day, these ETTs and Clara Fraser wrote letter after letter and memo after memo, documenting and protesting the ever-changing elements of the ETT program, as it continued to diverge from its original design.

By September 1974, the training, program oversight, and evaluation process of the ETT program had all changed. Why? "Vickery didn't like the Training Model—so evaluations forms once a month will be used instead," reported the ETT Planning Committee.[101] A class covering the fundamentals of electrical theory was announced, although whether it would be offered as an unpaid night class was still under dispute. The ETTs were then told "no comp time [would be] given to ETTs for schooling."[102] Finally, the class was put on hold. (It would be re-proposed in February 1975 and become even more contentious.)

A key element of the trainees' future with the utility was also revised. The ETTs would still be eligible for a Civil Service promotional exam after one year. But specifics about their training and pay relative to that of helpers were deferred to future contract negotiations with IBEW #77. These details were important because working as a helper was the traditional employment path into an apprenticeship.

At the time, apprenticeships lasted three years, but required a one year minimum of work experience as a helper, which then counted as the first year of an apprenticeship. In theory, it was fair that ETTs initially received significantly less pay than helpers because, unlike helpers, they would receive additional training and hands-on exposure to work in a variety of electrical trades and work sites. When these training elements were dropped, however, the ETTs were performing helper work for less pay.

Discussing even the possibility of increased wages for the ETTs triggered another round of power struggles between the City Light administration and the Public Service Careers program.

Concurrently, Clara Fraser sent a memo to her supervisor, Bill Rheubottom, requesting formal notification of her status with the ETT program. (Vickery had removed her as ETT coordinator more than two months earlier, in July.) Two days later, Rheubottom responded with a succinct memo informing Fraser she was no longer ETT program coordinator; he was.

In September, City Light employees organized a public rally to protest the mayor and city council's lack of response to the Public Review Committee's report on Vickery's management practices. (Both Uhlman and the council had been given the report on August 20.) The 11-member committee, established as part of the spring 1974 walkout settlement, had been charged to investigate Vickery's practices.

The majority of the Public Review Committee, while finding Vickery had not broken any laws and recommending he be retained as superintendent, called out two aspects of his behavior and administration. Vickery's "Public Attacks on Employees and Abuse of Human Dignity" required "immediate corrective action" and Vickery needed to be "admonished to make a public declaration of constructive efforts to correct the existing problems in human relationships."[103]

A minority report further called for Vickery to be fired for "violations of the City Charter, civil service procedures [and] his demonstrated record of consistent poor judgment and deficiencies in human interrelationships," and was signed by the two City Light employee representatives and James K. Bender, Executive Secretary of the King County Labor Council.[104]

Approximately 250 City Light employees attended the two-hour rally, including Clara Fraser and five of the ETTs—Jody Olvera, Jennifer Gordon, Megan Cornish, Teri Bach, Heidi Durham, and Margie

Wakenight. There is no record of a response from the city.

A few days later, Clara Fraser was profiled in the *Seattle Times* under the headline "Leader of City Light Revolt." The article summarized the way Fraser had unified the utility's workers:

> In the past few months, her speech has brought applause from City Light workers, many of whom scorned the anti-war demonstrators and look with suspicion upon any political party right or left of the basic two.[105]

Public outreach continued in October, with a panel discussion sponsored by the Feminist Coordinating Council, a coalition of Seattle-area feminist organizations. Held at the First African Methodist Episcopal Church, the discussion topic was discrimination and harassment at City Light. Clara Fraser chaired. ETT Daisy Jones and several other female City Light employees were speakers.

The city continued to stonewall not only the report from the Public Review Committee, but also the draft "Bill of Rights and Responsibilities" submitted by the elected, management-employee Bill of Rights and Responsibilities Committee. Personnel and Civil Service Director Jack Driscoll wrote his *own* version and demanded it replace the committee's document. The negotiating team that had settled the walkout (three electrical workers and three members of middle management) was once more allowed to mediate, and directed the BRRC to redraft and resubmit its proposal.

City Light administrators knew there were problems with the ETTs' work duties and pay relative to helpers. Management tried to come up with some way to make things look better before hearings on the ETT discrimination complaint moved forward. Specifics on how ETTs could become helpers would also be part of contract negotiations with IBEW #77 due to begin in less than a month. Walt Sickler, supervisor of Overhead Construction and a member of the ETT Working Subcommittee, did his best to take care of the matter by trying to fill helper positions before any ETTs could qualify.

Vickery's adjutant, Carole Coe, had her own way of further pressuring the ETTs. Without consulting the ETT committee, she issued a new City Light policy that reduced any possibility of extra or

"FEMINIST COORDINATING COUNCIL" PRESENTS A
PANEL DISCUSSION
ON

WOMEN WORKERS
AT CITY LIGHT

WEDNESDAY, OCT. 9, 1974
7:30 p.m.

PANELISTS

MARILYN BIRCHER, Accounting Technician
SHARON GEHRING, Intermediate Clerk
LOLA STEVENS, Sr. Clerk in Safety Dept.
DAISY JONES, Electrical Trades Trainee

FIRST A.M.E. CHURCH
(BASEMENT)

1522 14ᵗʰ AVE.

CHAIRPERSON

CLARA FRASER, City Light Education Coordinator

CHILDCARE PROVIDED

increased pay for the trainees. Contrary to existing practices, there would be no overtime for ETTs unless "the crew with which they are working is required to work overtime beyond the normal quitting time." They would not be allowed to work "scheduled overtime, evening call out, or weekend overtime."[106] This denied them valuable learning opportunities as well as being discriminatory. Megan Cornish later clarified: "Coe made sure the ETTs wouldn't be called at home to come to work overtime."[107]

It didn't matter whether the Personnel Department or City Light was in charge of ETT pay rates, because Coe also announced "it would be unwise to consider merit increases for the trainees." Instead, they would only receive "automatic six-month pay increases."[108]

Although Clara Fraser was no longer ETT coordinator, she went to bat for the women, writing Coe about "receiving calls from Trainees and Crew Chiefs opposing the new 'overtime policy.'"[109] Fraser also forwarded Coe's original memo to the ETT committee.

Then the ETTs were informed they would be rotated through the Overhead, Substation Construction, and Underground divisions within two weeks, and that once again their "training models" had been changed.

The ETTs met and authorized Heidi Durham to draft a protest letter on their behalf. On November 15 the letter was sent to Vickery, signed by every trainee except Patty Wong. Copies were sent to Rheubottom, Coe, Assistant Superintendent Whaley, Jack Driscoll (Personnel/Civil Service), IBEW #77, and the Working Subcommittee of the ETT committee.

It began, "We protest the discriminatory practices of City Light management and its broken promises to us," and went on:

> The only things that distinguish us from electrical helpers or apprentices are that we are far lower paid, get no special training, are not eligible for duties and benefits of other union members (such as overtime and clothing allowances), have unequal facilities, no voice about what happens to us, and no job security.[110]

The ETTs' letter also stated the women would send their own representative to the next meeting of the Working Subcommittee of the ETT committee, to deliver their list of urgent needs:

> 1. Equal overtime with other crew members, including overtime as an extension of the working day, scheduled overtime, and call-outs.
>
> 2. Merit and periodic pay increases to reach 95% of helper pay within one year of our hiring.
>
> 3. Equal facilities, including showers and drying rooms, immediately as required by law.
>
> 4. Promotional exam to apprentice or helper within one year of our hiring.
>
> 5. Classroom education on company time.
>
> 6. Clothing allowance.
>
> 7. Trainee representatives, with voice and vote, on all training committees.
>
> 8. Reinstatement of Clara Fraser as full-time coordinator and

advocate for the ETT Program.

9. Restoration of the Training Committees as decision-making—not advisory bodies.

10. Negotiate with [IBEW] Local 77 to waive the 6-month helper period before Overhead apprenticeship, since all trainees will already have spent one year doing essentially the same work as helpers.

11. Resurrect the original training model and insure regular, specific, and detailed progress reports.

12. Detailed job descriptions, defining what we can and cannot do and insuring that we can work and learn in each section we are assigned to.

13. Determine, along with Local 77, a concise and comprehensive definition of the relationship of trainee and helper job categories and apply that definition to our actual working conditions.

14. Human relations training, to provide training in progressive attitudes toward women, for *all* crew chiefs and supervisors with whom we will be involved.

15. Monthly trainee meetings on company time, to discuss problems and share information.[111]

The letter concluded that if "we do not see some of the above requests implemented and a schedule of when the others are to take effect," the ETTs would hold a press conference

> to let the public know what the Training Program is really like and that you are not giving us the training we and the public were led to believe we would receive.[112]

Vickery and his administrative minions were furious at the ETTs' "demands," as they called them. Vickery immediately sent a memo back to the women noting he had referred their requests to IBEW #77 for "further handling" as "subjects for collective bargaining,"[113] falsely assuming the union would support him. Heidi Durham, the ETTs' representative on the union's large negotiating team (as opposed to the smaller team that met with management), circulated both letters to union negotiators as they prepared for contract talks.

The next day, Walter Wheeles, Station Construction supervisor and member of the ETT Working Subcommittee, had an exchange with Durham at the utility's South Service Center. Durham recalled being told she might be laid off or "out on the street" and that "she and other trainees had no rights to ask for anything or demand anything."[114]

One may presume a happy Thanksgiving was had by all. The Monday after Thanksgiving, Carole Coe drafted a memo and sent it by courier to the six members of the ETT Working Subcommittee, asking them to sign it as their own message to Vickery. This they did, though three later regretted it or admitted they didn't know whether the allegations were true.[115] The letter attacked ETT "militancy," Fraser's "direction" over them, and her prior "affiliation," off-the-job, with several of the ETTs. Moreover, the letter claimed that the ETTs' actions were "damag[ing] the morale of the crews." It concluded that "the Trainees should agree to participate in the program as outlined...or step out of the program and make room for other persons."[116]

The "affiliation" Coe alluded to was Fraser, Durham, Cornish, and Bach's membership in Radical Women and FSP. The related innuendo, that this affiliation had in some way biased hiring the ETTs, had come up months before in Patty Wong's testimony before the Public Review Committee. And earlier in the fall, when Daisy Jones had gone to Joan Williams, City Light EEO officer, about racial slurs and on-the-job harassment, Jones was told "a lot of times we bring these problems on by association.... [Williams] felt the women were behind me, pushing me.... She told me...the guys didn't care for those women. They called them radical women or whatever."[117]

Vickery'd had enough. That Friday, December 6, he sent a letter to the ETTs, later referred to as his "loyalty oath":

> We are finding that internal dissention [sic] and unwillingness of the trainees to accept or follow management's decisions or directives pertaining to the program threatens to destroy the program and the concept.
>
> In view of this, then, I have decided to leave the decision to each

of you individually as to whether or not you care to continue on at City Light as an Electrical Trades Trainee. A decision to remain will necessitate your agreeing to participate in the program as outlined, defined and directed by the Lighting Department. Of course, any issues concerning negotiable items would continue to be handled by your union representative, and properly so.

Your response will be expected, in writing, no later than Wednesday, December 11th, 1974. Whether you decide to continue in the E.T.T. program or not, indicate your decision by filling in the proper response on the attached sheet, dating it, signing it, in *writing*, and return to me by the date shown.

If you do not care to continue on, we do have many others who are anxious to participate in this program.

A lack of response will be considered as a negative response and you will be discontinued from the E.T.T. program.[118]

The "attached sheet" had two paragraphs, each with a check box:

☐ YES, I have read the attached letter and have decided to remain in the ETT training program. I agree to participate in the program as outlined, defined and directed by the Lighting Department.
☐ NO, I do not care to continue in the City Light Electrical Trades Trainee program and my termination is effective immediately.[119]

Vickery's demand that the ETTs agree in advance to whatever training program City Light proposed, and that they do so in less than a week, would become a major rallying point for ETT support, as well as a critical element in the trainees' eventual legal victory.

Susan Magee, director of the Office of Women's Rights, immediately responded to Vickery's directive, informing him that

certainly, any termination of the trainees on the basis of this memo would be considered retaliation and processed accordingly under law.[120]

Vickery had also wrongly assumed IBEW #77 leadership would support him. But his ultimatum, if unchallenged, was a dangerous

The Trade Experience

"The trade experience requires a strong sense of personal responsibility. Tragedy is hovering over your shoulder always."
　　　　　　　　　　　　　　　　　　 – Matthew B. Crawford, Shop Class as Soulcraft

I wore a pair of new kid gloves
that wouldn't last a day
as the half inch hand line
burned through them,
up and down with the blocks,
the clamps, the come-alongs,
the wire, braces, lags,
the cross arms pushed off the edge
of the bucket high above—
whatever was cut away
and dropped down on the line
for me to catch
before it hit the ground.

I was mum my first month,
wide-eyed, a breath of air
that had never seen a gale,
a candle that had never seen a ball
of white hot flame engulf the pole
and the bucket on the arm
of the Hi-Ranger, never saw
the lineman lose his arms,
the apprentice, caught on a macho crew,
climbing without a safety strap
around the pole, fall
and break her back.

I have a badge of honor scar
from a smashed thumb
in the bushing shop,
a screw driver tip melted
black from short circuits,
a bad back. I vowed:
On my honor I will wear
the yellow hard hat, steel toed boots.
I'll use the warning tape, the red flags,

rubber goods, the safety belts, the gloves,
the masks, the sweaty Tyvek suits.
I promise to obey the rules
for switching power off and on.

Fraternities of high jinks
carried long days
with jokes and insults
thrown across the bench,
excuses made for no hard hat
or sleeves rolled up on a hot day,
with taunts across the yard that meant
when the crew chief comes,
or when you make a stupid move
I'll watch your back.

We didn't want to see
the journeyman dead
from the untested line he grabbed
that flung him from the tower,
a silhouette against the sun,
plunging to the steel deck.

No longer before our eyes
in the substation, the mayhem
on a darkened basement wall
where the wireman smoldered
years ago, after he went to work
on a live breaker across the room
by mistake.

But over our shoulders always.

by Joanne Ward,
retired as crew chief after 28 years in
electrical trades at Seattle City Light

precedent for all union members. IBEW #77 Business Representative Charlie Silvernale sent his own letter to each of the ETTs, counseling the women on how to respond to Vickery's loyalty oath:

> This local contacted its attorneys and has been advised that the memorandum be signed and dated as indicated in the memorandum and returned by the requested date.
>
> It was further recommended by our attorney not to indicate as prescribed in the letter yes or no.
>
> After you have signed and dated the document qualify it by the following sentence under your signature.
>
> I wish to remain in the Electrical Trades Trainee program providing all conditions are consistent with the Fair Employment Practices Ordinance.[121]

Gene Moen, the attorney for the ETTs and the Office of Women's Rights, recommended that the women also note on the form that they could not legally sign away their rights. Heidi Durham later gave her perspective on the local's actions:

> Support from the International Brotherhood of Electrical Workers (IBEW) Local 77 dwindled as time went on. But in the beginning, they were on our side. The union's support stemmed primarily from the fact that they themselves were at loggerheads with the same management at City Light as we were, so their biases melted away. It also helped that they were aware that they could also be sued, as other unions had been, if they stood against affirmative action.[122]

Opponents of the ETT program continued their barrage. On the same day Vickery sent out his loyalty oath, an anonymous letter from "a PO'd citizen" was sent to the utility, although it was not marked as received until the following week. "PO'd" accused ETT and Radical Women member Teri Bach and her Black co-worker of "fondling" on the job. Ken Hunich, director of Distribution, investigated, then sent a memo to Assistant Superintendent Whaley stating:

> The crew members deny any improper actions on their part....

The foreman of the crew...stated that he was positive that the character of the female trainee was above reproach in her relationships with male employees.[123]

This charge was then dropped, but Bach and other ETTs would face additional anonymous charges.

Carole Coe continued to spend a huge amount of her time undermining many aspects of the ETT program, ETT worksite issues, and especially Clara Fraser's work assignments. But Fraser challenged and organized resistance to Coe's administrative edicts and retaliations, whether they targeted Fraser or other City Light workers.

Gordon Vickery, the tyrannical superintendent of Seattle City Light.

Congratulations, You're Fired

By the beginning of 1975, City Light and its ETT program were a cauldron of mistrust and antagonism that boiled over into other labor-management disputes with the Uhlman administration and impacted Seattle at large. Most notably, the city firefighter's union led a signature-gathering campaign in a second attempt to recall Mayor Uhlman for

> violation of his oath of office in his appointment of Walter Hundley as the budget director, alleged by the union to be unqualified and incompetent, and budgetary actions that were detrimental to the fire department.[124]

Plenty of other city employees had their own reasons to want Uhlman out, without targeting Hundley, a former administrator in Seattle's anti-poverty program (where Clara Fraser worked under him), and one of the city's first Black administrators. These included those at City Light who had unsuccessfully organized the first Uhlman recall attempt, after the walkout. Many of the ETTs, Radical Women members, and Clara Fraser gathered signatures for this Uhlman recall campaign. (The attempt got on the July ballot but did not pass.)

In early January, Bill Rheubottom had issued the ETTs their first pay raises, ID cards, and city-employee driver's licenses. Two weeks later, he sent them a memo informing them of an upcoming Line Crew Helper/Apprentice Exam. He "strongly encourage[d]" the ETTs to "take the exam, if for nothing more than the experience of taking an exam of this kind."[125] Coe sent the ETTs her own memo the next day, echoing Rheubottom's comments.

Years later, Megan Cornish wryly explained, "We could take the test, but it wouldn't be a promotional exam for ETTs."[126] During the hearing on the women's discrimination case, Jack Driscoll (Personnel/Civil Service) and others would testify that

> trainees in other departments [than City Light] had normally taken promotional exams in order to be appointed to permanent positions.[127]

In another move to block the ETTs from becoming helpers, separate rosters for line crew helpers and other positions were combined. This meant there was a long and pre-existing list of men on the helper register *before* the ETTs could even take the test that might put them on that list. When the line crew helper test was given on March 1, all the ETTs took it, and all passed, but there was no longer a specific roster for the position.

A few weeks later, the trainees were informed there would be a basic electricity class that would start at the beginning of March and run until the end of May. Clara Fraser was assigned to organize the class although she was no longer the ETT coordinator.

In the previous ETT program for men of color, classes had been conducted during workdays, and the male trainees *were* paid for their class time. In designing the women's program, field supervisors had been clear that class time needed to be scheduled in all-day blocks or at night, so a workday would not be disrupted by a few hours of class time.

Now, some eight months after the women had entered the ETT program, they were directed to attend an electrical theory class. But it would be held at night, without pay. Many of the ETTs refused to participate because, although apprentices took night classes without pay, the women's wages were significantly less.

Administrative discrimination also continued in regard to physical accommodations. In March, Clara Fraser wrote Coe on behalf of the ETTs to protest that they still did not have the restroom and shower facilities legally mandated, although the June 1974 ETT "Fact Sheet" had clearly stated:

> State law requires separate facilities for each sex; where rest rooms are currently available for males, similar facilities need to be

supplied for females. Dual rest rooms are not necessarily mandatory if one facility can be *used* separately. Where no facilities are
provided for men, none need be supplied for women. City Light
will furnish whatever facilities are needed to satisfy state law and
Title VII of the Civil Rights Act, which mandates "equal" facilities.

Change Rooms will likewise be provided or partitioned.[128]

At the end of March, City Light received an anonymous letter
charging the ETTs assigned to the Underground Division—Jody Olvera, Teri Bach, and Megan Cornish—with drinking on the job with
other crew members. All in fact were careful to be squeaky clean,
because they knew they were under special surveillance. Five men
admitted to drinking and were suspended. On April 8, Walt Sickler,
who had recently worked to keep ETTs off the helper roster, interviewed each of the three women separately. No disciplinary action
was taken.

But Bach, who answered questions but vehemently protested
being grilled about charges from an anonymous source, was suspended for three days for "willful violation of legitimate directions
given you by a supervisor."[129] This was actually because she challenged Sickler's directives while being interviewed about the anonymous claim.

At this point another party voiced its opinion that Bach's suspension was simple harassment. Susan Magee, director of the Office of
Women's Rights, weighed in with a letter to Vickery that characterized Bach's suspension as part of a "pattern of retaliation."[130]

That same day, Bach and IBEW #77's Silvernale met with the
supervisor who had suspended her. The supervisor told them the
memo suspending her "had not been written by him."[131] Within
a day Cornish, Bach, and Durham wrote and circulated a letter
among the union's members, making clear the attack on Bach in-
fringed upon the rights of all City Light workers. Some 100 IBEW
#77 members signed it, voicing their objection to the interrogations
and suspensions of IBEW #77 members on drinking charges on the
basis of anonymous letters.

Although unsigned, the anonymous letter used terminology

such as job classification titles that the general public would not be familiar with. According to Megan Cornish, crews later surmised that an underground helper was the author of the letter, in part because of his sudden promotion to journey-level status after years of failing exams.[132]

When the union didn't take immediate action, Teri Bach filed her own grievance. With that, IBEW #77's Silvernale forwarded Bach's grievance to Joe Recchi, the utility's assistant superintendent, and requested Bach's suspension be rescinded.

City Light fought back. Carole Coe urged the local to "carefully consider that the Department's decision was appropriate and just…. We trust that…the grievance [will be] dismissed by you…."[133] Only then did Vickery respond to the Office of Women's Rights' two-week-old letter, explaining that the investigation of Bach was still underway, and that her suspension was merited.

All the ETTs had taken the line crew helper Civil Service test in March. On May 1, results were announced and all of them had passed. This sparked an amendment to the ETTs' discrimination complaint because manipulations to the roster had made their test results fairly irrelevant. Jody Olvera, Jennifer Gordon, and Letha Neal were added as formal complainants. Margie Wakenight, who had sensed impending layoffs and returned to work in the City Light administration building in mid-March, was dropped. The content of the complaint was also expanded:

> 1) Denial of "on-time" training previously provided similarly situated male Electrical Trades Trainees.
>
> 2) Denial of equal pay for equal work. In the absence of "on-time" training we perform substantially similar work under substantially similar conditions as do Helpers all of whom are male and we receive a lower rate of pay.
>
> 3) Denial of opportunities to be employed as Line Crew Helpers because of the substantial number of Helpers hired by City Light after June 24, 1974 up until 3/10/75 from a Civil Service register established 9/20/71 which contained no women. A new Civil Service exam was given on 3/10/75 which all of us passed.

Further, we charge that City Light has retaliated against us in a variety of ways including denial of "on-time" training because trainees filed a sex discrimination complaint against the department prior to this amended complaint. Such actions are a violation of Seattle Ordinance 102562 as amended.[134]

That same week, Heidi Durham filed a grievance against the utility "on behalf of myself and all the Electrical Trades Trainees," citing two sections of the union contract: one explicitly banning discrimination, and the other citing mandatory "clothing allowance, and compensatory time for classroom training" as conditions of federal funding paid to the city.[135] (No federal money was spent directly on the ETT program, but federal requirements that accompanied other federal funds applied to *all* of Seattle's programs.)

No immediate action was taken on this grievance and City Light still refused to rescind Bach's suspension.

Then, just before Memorial Day weekend, Carole Coe sent a letter to each of the ETTs. Her letter would become infamous for its cheery notice that the women trainees would be out of work as of June 24, 1975. Several ETTs later characterized Coe's message as "Congratulations, you're fired." Wrote Coe:

> As the anniversary date of the implementation of the Electrical Trades Trainee Program at City Light approaches, Management is in the process of reviewing the program as to its successes and failures, as well as possibilities for future training programs of this type.
>
> It is appropriate to say, at this point, that the ETT program has served its purpose in that each of you has taken and passed a Civil Service examination for Lineman Helper/Apprentice and your names are on the eligible register.
>
> The objective of the ETT program was to prepare women to compete in Civil Service exams for apprentice or helper in the electrical trades, with the purpose of providing equal employment opportunities for women in the electrical utility field, and with the entry of your names on a Civil Service eligible register, we feel our goals have been accomplished.
>
> We congratulate you on this accomplishment![136]

Coe's conclusion, that "the ETT program has served its purpose" once the trainees' names were "on a Civil Service eligible register," was simply wrong. The goal of the program was *not* to get ETTs onto a roster. As early as August 1973, when City Light was first considering such a program, the director of Public Service Careers, Richard Burt, identified its goal as

> the placement of each individual in an apprenticeship program with one year's advance standing [eligibility].[137]

In June 1974, the ETT program "Fact Sheet" stated that the goal of the program was "To employ and train 10 women as electrical workers."[138]

The ETTs immediately protested Coe's memo and won a 90-day extension of their jobs.

Coe then pushed the utility's position in a letter to Barbara Carter, investigator for the Office of Women's Rights. She claimed

> ETTs understood program would last only one year and that the purpose was to train them to take a Helper Exam

Freedom Socialist

Press conference to protest layoff of ETTs. From left, Jody Olvera, Jennifer Gordon, Megan Cornish, Teri Bach, Angel Arrasmith, Heidi Durham.

Their continuing in the trade depends on

a. Capabilities and attitudes

b. Opportunities in competitive situation[139]

But Coe's assertions were false.

The ETT program had been designed as a two-year program, as was highly documented, almost from its inception. The non-promotional Civil Service test, which the trainees had taken with approximately 500 others, only put them on a roster for future consideration at such time as there *were* helper openings.

One week later, the ETTs met with IBEW #77 representatives to present a draft of the letter they wanted the local to send to Vickery. They and the union agreed

that Union would make 3 requests of ETTs nonnegotiable demands—no layoffs of ETTs, Hire ETTs as Helpers and promotional exam for all ETTs.[140]

(IBEW #77's contract with City Light was still in negotiation. In August, the local would send portions of the trainees' letter to Seattle's director of Personnel, Jack Driscoll.)

Day-to-day retaliation of the ETTs continued. On June 13, Daisy Jones sent a memo to her line crew foreman, Frank Karabach, who was infamous for his bigotry and mistreatment of crew members:

Objecting to her unsubstantiated low evaluation she received from Crew chief and members from the crew [and]

...Requests that she receive an unbiased evaluation and be transferred to another crew where she can get fair treatment[141]

On July 1, the recall election to remove Uhlman failed. Vickery immediately stepped up his attack on Fraser and the ETT program, using departmental budget cuts. On Friday, July 11, Clara Fraser was called into Employee Relations Manager Donald Winkley's office and told she was laid off

under the 5 percent budget reduction because she was a provisional employee. He told her she was to leave immediately, turn in her identification card, and not return the next week.[142]

The following Monday, Vickery made an announcement to City Light workers that there would be a 100-employee reduction through "retirements, normal transfers and resignations....[and] limited lay-offs."[143] Testimony during Fraser's legal challenge would prove she was the *only* person permanently laid off. (Several helpers were temporarily laid off, but then rehired approximately six months later.)

On August 6, a year and a day after the ETTs filed their discrimination complaint, the utility hired two ETTs, Patty Wong and Jennifer Gordon, as line crew helpers. Wong was the only female trainee who never supported or joined the ETTs' discrimination complaint. Gordon was one of the top-scoring participants of any gender on the Civil Service proficiency test. Gordon remembered her hiring as a helper was

> just as bizarre as every other step along the way had been, including my good scores on a test that was wildly different from other tests we had taken.... My world changed for the worse when everybody else got laid off....that put me in an odd position. Being hired when they were laid off created a huge additional wrinkle separating me from other ETTs....
>
> I got onto a horrendous big crew, and they were out to get me. But they still would have been incredibly hostile if I had been male, that was the culture.[144]

Two days after Gordon was hired, the *Seattle Times* ran a long article, "Sparks Fly Over Training Program," attempting to summarize the history and current status of the ETT program, City Light's "landmark electrical-trades training program for women....scheduled to end September 24."[145]

The *Seattle Times* article noted that two ETTs were now helpers. It then discussed the two previous anonymous complaints against Teri Bach and her refutation of all charges, citing the assertion by the Office of Women's Rights that Bach's suspension was retaliation. It also mentioned that Margie Wakenight and Daisy Jones (both single mothers, with Jones supporting five children) "had since left the program for other jobs." (For details on what became of the original ten ETTs, see Appendix 1, ETT Close-ups.)

The *Times* also gave former ETT Patty Wong, now a helper, ample opportunity to criticize both the program and the other trainees, and to reassert she was being used as a "pawn." In the same article, Carole Coe made her case for City Light management:

> "We've never promised anyone a job out of the program.... We wanted to prepare them to compete in what was essentially a man's field."
>
> Ms. Coe said the trainees may well be able to find jobs with other electrical utilities in the region. Nor have they been scratched off the list of candidates for City Light helper's positions, should the jobs open up.[146]

Heidi Durham tried to clarify the situation:

> Management hasn't accepted its responsibility for affirmative action. After they spent money on training us, they're going to turn some of us out on the street.[147]

Vickery got the final word in the article:

> When asked if City Light will continue with some type of women's training program...Vickery said, "I don't know. Maybe we will, maybe we won't.... I'm happy that we have achieved the major objective of the program, which was to give them an extra advantage in preparing for the Civil Service examination for helper."[148]

The *Seattle Times* article did not, however, mention a major event in the ETTs' discrimination case. The Office of Women's Rights had issued Findings of Fact supporting the ETTs' claims. Barbara Carter, the OWR investigator on the complaint, also outlined the standard process for resolving a finding of discrimination:

> Reasonable cause having been found to believe that violations of Seattle Ordinance 102562, as amended, have occurred, and that all of the charges are true, I now invite you to engage in an effort to achieve a just resolution of this matter through conference and conciliation.[149]

On August 20, the OWR sent a letter to City Light requesting immediate conciliation. Three weeks later, Vickery responded with a letter refusing to conciliate and outlining his objections. He and his staff were not pleased with the OWR's investigative process and findings, which he claimed *"without exception"* were:

> 1. Unprofessional in the manner in which the investigation of the charges was conducted;
> 2. Some "Findings of Fact" were of questionable basis, with some statements taken [out of] context and/or;
> 3. Some of the statements made are pure fabrication....
>
> Because of the completely unproven allegations contained in both the charges and the findings of fact and our own subsequent research into the circumstances described in these documents, we [City Light] do not desire to conciliate this case and Electrical Trades Trainees will be terminated on September 24, as we indicated to you previously.[150]

The protesting ETTs sent out their own press release the following day, pointing out that the OWR's Findings of Fact were

> in our favor on all 4 counts:
> 1. Discriminatory denial of training and associated benefits
> 2. Failure to provide for equal pay for equal work
> 3. Discriminatory failure to hire
> 4. Retaliation/harassment against the ETTs[151]

The conflict continued to make headlines. A *Seattle Times* article on September 11, "Vickery Blasts Sex-Bias Charge," described Vickery's refusal to conciliate, and quoted OWR Director Susan Magee's observation that respondents to discrimination charges often "try to discredit the findings."[152]

The September 11 *Seattle Post-Intelligencer's* front-page coverage reported on a scheduled meeting between the women's rights office and the utility, and pointed out that if conciliation attempts failed, the next step would be a hearing before a city examiner and panel. A week later, a mayor's aide told the *Post-Intelligencer* that "nothing has changed, formally" as a result of a four-hour meeting with representatives of the mayor's office, City Light, and the Office of

Women's Rights.[153]

And with that, the trainees were abruptly terminated. They had known September 24 was the date City Light had been using for when the ETT program would end, but it had not been clear the utility would act. On September 23, they received a formal layoff letter from Vickery, to take effect the next day.

> We feel we have accomplished our objective and, as Carole Coe pointed out to you in her memorandum of May 28, 1975, we do congratulate each of you on your individual accomplishments in the program....
>
> Because we have engaged in exhaustive discussions over the past three-four weeks with representatives of Women's Rights and the Mayor's Office in an effort to arrive at some equitable resolution of your outstanding charges of sex discrimination, we were unable to give you formal notice of termination until the final day of the extension period. We had hoped some agreement could be reached. None was. As a result, we are enclosing your Personnel Action Form, indicating your employment with the Lighting Department in our Electrical Trades Trainee Program ends with close of the work day at 5:00 p.m., September 24, 1975. We are including two weeks additional salary on your pay warrant in lieu of two weeks formal notice of termination, although, of course, you did have knowledge of when the program would end.
>
> Your name will remain on the Civil Service eligible list and there may be future opportunities for employment from that list.[154]

A pat on the back, and don't let the door hit you on the way out. An attached memo from Vickery added insult to the injury. He had "received a call" from the Personnel/Civil Service Department, which had received word from the comptroller, who had received an opinion from the city's legal counsel

> that any form of severance pay is not allowable and this would be an illegal payment. Consequently, we are not able to pay two weeks additional salary we proposed to pay.[155]

The Feminist Coordinating Council immediately sent a letter to "the Feminist Community" asking supporters of affirmative action to write Mayor Uhlman and send letters to the editor to call for reinstatement of the ETTs and continuation of the ETT program.

It would take nine months for the ETT case to move through the hearings process. The women continued this legal battle as they worked other jobs.

Bach, Cornish, and Durham continued to work in the electrical trade while laid off, at first in a residential wiring apprenticeship with IBEW #46, which was trying to break into what was then a non-union field. Local #46 next sent Teri Bach to the Trident submarine base, on Hood Canal, to do commercial wiring. (As a federal job site, it didn't require commercial licenses from its workers.)

The specter of an influx of female electricians was intended as leverage to get the employer to hire back some laid-off union members. Bach and the union agreed that in trade for her help she'd get training from her male co-workers. The employer settled rather than have more women on the worksite. The male unionists were rehired. But Bach's hard work led to Cornish and Durham also being hired at the base.[156]

There was new misery for the electrical workers still at City Light. Contract negotiations between IBEW #77 and the utility failed and these workers went out on strike October 17, 1975. They stayed out until January 23, 1976, in the longest public workers strike in Washington history. But it was a strike that ultimately had to settle for management's original offer. (See Appendix 2 for a fuller description of this strike.)

In April 1976, the ETTs' case finally went before a municipal hearings officer and three-member hearings panel. Attorney Gene Moen, who represented the ETTs and the Office of Women's Rights, remembered there were a number of times the parties had to establish procedures since every other previous discrimination complaint in the city had been resolved before going to hearing.

Deputy Hearing Examiner John Hendrickson issued his proposed findings and decision on June 9, 1976, with an order citing discrimination by City Light on two counts. However, "Regarding all other allegations, the charging parties have failed to maintain

Victorious ETTs celebrate with Office of Women's Rights staff. From left, staff-person and former acting director Marya Sharer, Teri Bach, director Audrey Olsen, investigator Barbara Carter, Heidi Durham, Megan Cornish.

their burden of proof and the remainder of the complaints should be dismissed."[157]

But the three-member hearings panel had final say. It almost completely reversed Hendrickson's recommendation, issuing its decision a month later on July 9. The ETTs had won their case!

City Light was ordered to pay back wages as well as "the differential between 'trainee' and 'helper' salaries." It was required to "cease and desist from any and all unlawful employment practices," to hire Arrasmith, Bach, Durham, Cornish and Neal as helpers and to admit them into the City Light apprenticeship program within six months.[158]

In addition, for two years, the Office of Women's Rights would monitor

> (1) City Light's record in hiring women for skilled trades, and
> (2) any future disciplinary action against the ETTs.[159]

"Women Win Back Pay from City Light" was the headline of the *Seattle Times* article that announced the decision. Heidi Durham was jubilant:

> I've known that all along for two years I was right. It's great. Now I can become an electrician.[160]

Mike Sharar, City Light spokesperson, was more guarded, and "declined to say whether the utility would appeal."

In a later interview with the *Freedom Socialist*, Durham

> attribute[d] the stunning victory to the solidarity of the trainees, the support from IBEW Local 77 and hundreds of other City Light workers, the assistance of feminists and Office of Women's Rights staff workers and attorney, intense public interest, and general disgust with the Uhlman-Vickery stripe of venal politician.[161]

The panel's decision became the OWR's binding order, issued on August 19, 1976. In it, eight of the ETTs were collectively awarded $120,000 in back pay and damages. Margie Wakenight (now married and using the name Bellinger), had transferred to a clerk position in the substation engineering department before the ETT program was terminated and received no financial award, although she later returned to the trades as a substation operator. Only one ETT, Patty Wong, was not part of the complaint settlement since she had claimed there was no discrimination (though she negotiated a separate back-pay settlement with management).

Two former trainees, Daisy Jones and Jennifer Gordon, received a back-pay settlement, but were no longer working at City Light. Daisy Jones had taken a job driving bus for Metro Transit as soon as the ETT program was terminated, in order to support her large family. Jennifer Gordon had been hired as a helper, and so had not been laid off with the other ETTs. She quit City Light during the 1975-76 strike, exhausted by the isolation and unremitting harassment she experienced as the only feminist helper.

Six women were also awarded reinstatement and retroactive promotion to electrical helper positions: Angel Arrasmith, Teri Bach, Megan Cornish, Heidi Durham, Letha Neal, and Jody Olvera. They returned to City Light with the option, in theory, of entering one of City Light's apprenticeship programs within six months.

But the ETTs' legal victory didn't mean that harassment and discrimination were eliminated at City Light or elsewhere in the city departments.

Months before the ETTs returned to work, six women had been hired by the Seattle Fire Department in another attempt at affirmative action. Within two months, five of the recruits resigned under threat of firing, which would have barred them from the next firefighter recruitment class. Lori Lakshas, the last female holdout (and a member of Radical Women at the time) was fired. She filed a complaint with the Office of Women's Rights, which found in her favor in 1979, although the case was not resolved until June 1984.

Clara Fraser on speaking tour about her discrimination case against City Light.

The People v. City Light

> I'm not even the defendant—I'm the Charging Party, the plain-
> tiff. Nevertheless, I'm the one who ends up on trial, with my virtue,
> past practices and motives subject to a smear campaign.[162]
>
> –Clara Fraser

Former ETT program coordinator Clara Fraser filed her discrimination claim on August 5, 1974, the same day as the ETTs. But while
their complaint was resolved in nine months, Fraser's case took
seven long years. Unlike the ETTs, Fraser charged discrimination on
the basis of political ideology as well as sex discrimination. This put
her case under the jurisdiction of Seattle's Human Rights Department, rather than the Office of Women's Rights.

Fraser's initial claim against the City of Seattle and City Light
stated:

> I became an employee of City Light on June 4, 1973. In Septem-
> ber of 1973 I was put in charge of the proposed Electrical Trainee
> Program for women. On June 24, 1974 the women trainees started
> work for City Light. On July 9, I was precipitously informed that I
> was relieved of any connection with the Trainee Program. I believe
> that I was discriminated against on the basis of my sex and politi-
> cal ideology.[163]

Once Fraser and the ETTs filed their complaints, the torrent of
memos between Coe, Rheubottom, the trainees, and Fraser created
a paper trail that would eventually help Fraser win her case.

One issue that would be contested in Fraser's hearings was the
first training event Fraser had worked on after her removal as ETT
coordinator, a human relations workshop. ("Human relations" was
the term used for training that gave employees, especially man-

agement, specific ways and insights about how to meet worksite requirements and policies of affirmative action and Equal Employment Opportunity, or EEO, law.) After she had designed it, Fraser's workshop had been summarily reassigned to the city Personnel Department. It was then cancelled shortly before Fraser filed her discrimination claim. On the day Fraser filed, Carole Coe sent a memo to EEO Officer Joan Williams documenting Fraser had spent money planning this workshop without conducting it.

Throughout the fall of 1974 and into that winter, Coe and sometimes Bill Rheubottom (Coe's underling and Fraser's boss), continued to micro-manage Fraser's time and work. In one memo, Coe reprimanded Fraser for a letter written four months previously. Coe then denied Fraser's "extra" pay for supervisory duties Coe had assigned to her during an absence by Rheubottom.

Meanwhile, Vickery and Coe devised a plan that would resolve both their ongoing difficulties with Clara Fraser and a five percent departmental budget reduction: cut funding to the ETT program and the Training Division.

On May 13, 1975, Fraser's job was secretly deleted from the upcoming 1976 budget and replaced by a new position, "Manpower Development Specialist." Since this was a "new" position, it would require a new Civil Service exam. Coe worked with the city Personnel Department to shape this exam.

Around May 19, Fraser was notified she would have to take the new exam, competing with others for her existing job. She immediately amended her discrimination complaint to include this custom Civil Service exam as job retaliation. The Civil Service Commission reviewed the proposed test and voted to make the exam "noncompetitive" for incumbents. This meant Fraser, the sole incumbent, would have only to pass the exam to retain her job.

Realizing the test wouldn't get rid of Fraser, Vickery selectively applied his budget cut. On Friday, July 11, Fraser was laid off without notice at 4:30 p.m. because of a five percent "reduction in force."

On the next workday, Vickery announced that 100 current positions would be eliminated through attrition. As it turned out, Fraser was the only administrative or professional staff person terminated under this reduction.

IBEW Local #77 passed a resolution in support of Fraser and informed the Civil Service Commission it had done so. The next week, Fraser requested a hearing with that commission. Meanwhile, Vickery notified Office of Women's Rights Director Susan Magee that he refused to settle the ETT case without going to hearing. A month later, at the end of September, the program was terminated and all but two ETTs were laid off.

In another act of retaliation, Clara Fraser's unemployment compensation was withheld and she was ordered to refund the severance pay she had already received. Fraser didn't take this lying down. She protested publicly, and the order was dropped.

Vickery then blocked Fraser from receiving further unemployment benefits, petitioning the city council to reduce the city's unemployment payments to anyone who received state benefits. The council agreed and Fraser's unemployment compensation stipend was cut in half. There is no record anyone else's unemployment claim was affected. Fraser again amended her discrimination claim to include these retributions.

In the midst of this, on October 17, 1975, IBEW #77 went out on its lengthy strike.

Late in 1975, results from the "non-competitive" Civil Service exam for Fraser's job were made public. Most of the test scores were erratic, so Fraser and others who had taken the test filed a protest with the Civil Service Commission. Personnel denied Fraser's challenge while granting adjustments to the other applicants. Shortly afterwards, on January 23, 1976, IBEW #77's strike ended. City Light workers returned, having taken a huge hit on the contract that was signed.

Six months later, in June 1976, only a few weeks before the ETTs' discrimination case was finally settled, Fraser's former job, officially a new position, was filled by a male who had far less experience. The fact that the position was filled quickly reinforced the view that Fraser's layoff was a pretext for discrimination.

It took another year, until May 24, 1977, for Human Rights Department investigator Joel Salmi to issue his findings and conclusions on the Fraser case. Salmi found violations of Seattle's Fair Employment Practices Ordinance in all six of the allegations Fraser had filed:

A. Removal as Coordinator of the Female ETT Program
...the Charging Party [Fraser] was removed...because of her sex and her political ideology and because she opposed unfair employment practices....

B. Reduction of Duties and Assignments
...the Respondent [Seattle City Light] limited and reduced the Charging Party's job duties and assignments because of her sex and political ideology, and in retaliation for filing a discrimination complaint and opposing unfair employment practices.

C. Termination from Employment
...the Respondent knowingly and willfully terminated the Charging Party from employment because of her sex and political ideology, and in retaliation for filing discrimination complaints.

D. Method of Termination
...the Respondent used a different method of terminating the Charging Party than that used for other employees because of her political ideology and in retaliation for filing discrimination complaints.

E. Civil Service Classification and Examination of the Charging Party's Position
...the Respondent knowingly and willfully caused a civil service exam to be developed and administered which adversely impacted the Charging Party because of her sex and political ideology and in retaliation for filing discrimination complaints, and...knowingly and willfully denied the Charging Party the opportunity to be reinstated in her position because of her sex and political ideology and in retaliation for filing discrimination complaints.

F. Other Terms and Conditions of Employment
...the Charging Party was treated differently with respect to the terms and conditions of her employment because of her sex and political ideology and in retaliation for filing discrimination complaints and for opposing unfair employment practices.[164]

A discrimination determination includes an offer to conciliate. On August 9, Human Rights Department Director Vivian Caver sent notice to Mayor Uhlman and the heads of the two departments charged with discrimination, City Light Superintendent Vickery and Personnel/Civil Service Director Jack Driscoll, that attempts to settle the case had failed. She notified the mayor that he had the option to "request that further conciliation be held."[165] There is no record how, or if, Uhlman responded.

About the same time Uhlman passed up this opportunity to settle Fraser's case, he decided to run for governor of Washington rather than a third term as mayor of Seattle. He didn't make it through the primary.

Charles Royer, a former TV newscaster, was elected Seattle's new mayor. Both he and the other front-runner, Paul Schell, had promised as part of their mayoral campaigns to fire Vickery. But when Royer

Understanding Political Discrimination

The charge of ideological discrimination was based on management's hostility to Clara Fraser as an openly radical advocate for women, people of color and workers at the utility.

An armchair socialist would probably have been tolerated. But Fraser lived her politics in the inner sanctum of the workplace.

She was a visible and outspoken critic of management abuses during the walkout, during her participation on the Bill of Rights and Responsibilities Committee, in everyday interactions in the Training Division, and in the recall efforts against Superintendent Gordon Vickery and Mayor Wes Uhlman. The frequent red-baiting smears against her were an attempt to divide her from other workers at the utility. They also revealed management's highly political ire.

In her case against City Light, Fraser also charged sex discrimination because the common accusations against her as being "abrasive," "defiant," "controlling," etc., reflected a deep discomfort at a *woman* exhibiting strong traits that would have been tolerable in a male.

Part of Fraser's ideology was her feminism, and part of the hostility against her was because she was a *woman* radical.

–Helen Gilbert, Red Letter Press

took office on January 1, 1978, he found out Vickery had some sort of contract that could not be broken, lasting through 1978 or 1979 (records differ).

From September 1977 through May 1979, a string of motions, appeals, legal challenges, and delays from the city's legal counsel kept Fraser's case from moving forward. Newly elected Mayor Royer tried to settle Fraser's case. In early June 1978, he sent a memo to Vickery and Human Rights Department Director Vivian Caver that began by itemizing the estimated cost to the city if the hearings process took place:

> The total cost to the City of the hearing regardless of the outcome, would be $67,000. Most of these costs are "hidden," but the impact on the taxpayer is nevertheless very great.[166]

Royer then summarized the settlements proposed by City Light and HRD:

> The Lighting Department asserts that the issue should be settled at "nuisance value" alone, while the Department of Human Rights is seeking about $40,000 in back pay and reinstatement for Ms. Fraser.[167]

Royer's letter directed terms for a settlement:

> On the basis of my review, the Department of Lighting is directed to settle this issue with the Human Rights Department on the basis of the following:
> 1. The Department of Lighting will pay Ms. Fraser $25,000.
> 2. There will be no reinstatement as part of the settlement.
> 3. The consent agreement settling this case should include a standard phrase stating that City Light does not admit to any wrongdoing, but is agreeing to settle in order to avoid the continued costs of litigation.[168]

There is no further record of Royer's settlement attempt, which suggests the offer never made it out of the city's internal processes.

In the meantime, Vickery made plans to leave City Light. He was nominated as head of the U.S. Fire Administration, under President

Jimmy Carter, and received the appointment. He left the utility in late 1978 or early 1979.

Royer immediately sought a new City Light superintendent and picked Robert Murray, "an Oregon energy consultant."[169] Randy Revelle, then chair of the city's Utilities Committee, fiercely opposed Murray's appointment.

> Revelle supported his position [against Murray's appointment] with affidavits from [Murray's former] employers and the fact that Murray had never supervised more than 10 people and had never fired anyone. City Light was the nation's fourth largest public utility and employed 1900, one third of the city's workforce.[170]

The Seattle City Council eventually confirmed Murray in May, with a one-vote margin.

Weeks later, Royer tried again to settle Clara Fraser's case. This time his proposed settlement got acceptance from all the necessary parties: City Light, the Human Rights Department, and Fraser herself. Final terms were drafted by City Attorney Doug Jewett, and signed by Seattle Human Rights Commission President Marlaina Kiner and Seattle Women's Commission President Shirley Skellenger. The terms were: no admission of wrongdoing by the city, $30,000 in damages to Fraser, and a bona fide job offer for Fraser at City Light.

Stunningly, when the settlement came before the City Council for approval on July 2, the council rejected it six-to-two. Only Norm Rice and Sam Smith, the two Black councilmen, voted for settlement. Councilwoman Jeanette Williams, a longtime supporter of the Human Rights Department, was out of town for the vote.

When later covering Fraser's hearings, a *Seattle Sun* reporter asked rhetorically:

> Since discrimination cases are generally settled without a hearing, why was the settlement vetoed? Council member Norm Rice, backed by Sam Smith, said he thought a settlement would "save the city some money."....
>
> According to Hugh Spitzer, counsel to the mayor "Miller and

The Ballad of Clara Fraser

By Patrick Haggerty

Thank you, Carol Coe, my clever
  blonde bombshell
For digging up the scuttlebutt and
  tarnish.
So her attitude is cranky,
So there's been some hanky-panky
With a trainee by the name of Megan
  Cornish.
So the chair of the Bill of Rights
  Committee
Is a Trotskyite and a Marxist albatross.
She nixed my negative action plan
When she cut my throat on the
  witness stand.
Ms. Coe, you got to show her who's
  the boss.

CHORUS: Clara Fraser, Clara Fraser
The proper rules of etiquette don't
  phase her.
She's a commie, she's a dyke,
And her politics ain't lady-like.
I just can't stand her abrasive behavior.

Now I know, Ms. Coe, it ain't exactly
  cricket
To spy on your employees while they
  picket.
But for the sake of her transition,
Not to mention your position
Get her FBI file, and quick step it.
Now when she joined the linemen in
  the walkout
She threw the central building in a
  dither.
She's a striker, a wage hiker,
She's the steno pool's Pied Piper.
Every file clerk and typer walked out
  with her.

CHORUS: Clara Fraser, Clara Fraser
Let's print up a phony leaflet to
  disgrace her.
She's a commie, she's a dyke,
And her politics ain't lady-like.
I just can't stand her abrasive behavior.

Thank you, Carol Coe, my clever
  hatchet girl.
You're the Margaret Thatcher of City
  Light.
You came up with the perfect
  scam,
The five-percent reduction plan,
We'll just lay her off without a fight.
She never would sign my oath of
  loyalty
'Cause she loves Karl Marx more than
  she loves me.
So, Ms. Coe go give the axe to Clara
  Fraser
That's an order from King George
  Gordon Vickery.

CHORUS: Clara Fraser, Clara Fraser
Her tongue is sharper than my Gillette
  razor.
She's a commie, she's a dyke,
And her politics ain't lady-like.
I just can't stand her abrasive behavior.

Clara Fraser, Clara Fraser
I doubt that Jesus Christ himself could
  save her.
She's a commie, she's a dyke,
And her politics ain't lady-like.
I just can't stand her abrasive behavior.
CLARA FRASER!

Hill opposed the settlement because they didn't like the department getting rid of a problem with a cash settlement."

"Ms. Fraser's case brought out one of the basic problems with human rights cases," Spitzer said. "A hearing will legally determine whether or not there was discrimination. Although the city stands to lose more money, this is preferable to simply brushing off the issue with a cash settlement."

Fraser believes the veto was "an attempt to injure and halt the whole process of equal employment opportunity."[171]

In mid-September, the city council appropriated a total of $21,000 for the immediate expenses of Fraser's hearing, $13,500 to the Human Rights Department to hire an outside attorney, and $7,500 for the hearing examiner's salary—already spending $12,000 more than the proposed settlement amount.

The hearings on Fraser's discrimination complaint began on January 14, 1980. The Human Rights Department and Fraser were represented by John Chen Beckwith. Dona Cloud, from the City Attorney's Office, represented City Light. Attorney Sally Pasette had been appointed *pro tempore* hearing examiner, and a hearing panel of three women had also been appointed.

The *Seattle Times* ran an article, "Fireworks Expected in Bias-Suit Hearing," at the end of the first week of hearings, mocking one department of the city suing another:

> The city can't lose in a discrimination suit now being argued before a city hearing-examiner board, but it could likely be an expensive victory.[172]

Fraser's lawyer led witnesses through exhaustive testimony that laid out her political views, her well-known activist history, her mobilizing for affirmative action and workers' rights. He also documented numerous incidents where the Vickery administration relentlessly retaliated, attacked her professionalism, and treated Fraser disparately because of her commitment to the ETT program and other City Light workers.

This included the testimony of Willene Guillory, former Training

Unit secretary, that Vickery had told one of his staff

> Clara was a good old girl. If she was only as dedicated to him
> or City Light as she is to Karl Marx, she would make a good em-
> ployee.[173]

After two weeks, the hearing adjourned for a month. Fraser supporters held a press conference during the interim, and the Freedom Socialist Party issued a special edition of the *Freedom Socialist* newspaper that compiled details of Fraser's case to date.

When hearings resumed, City Light attorney Dona Cloud began by asserting the utility did not discriminate on the basis of Fraser's political ideology. "'Political ideology'...means beliefs about management of government, not management of a utility."[174] During the next three months of testimony, City Light bosses had shifting rationales for the actions it had taken against Fraser. Her former co-worker and supervisor, Bill Rheubottom, took the stand and brought new charges against her. As reported by Don McGaffin, the KING-TV reporter and editorialist who chronicled the hearings:

> Bill Rheubottom said someone in his office read his memos.
> Someone took or hid his work assignments causing him to be
> berated by his boss [Carole Coe]. And since there were only two
> others in that office, Clara Fraser and another woman, well....
>
> Fraser's attorney John Chen Beckwith looked like he might leap
> over his table.
>
> Did Rheubottom have evidence Clara Fraser hid work assign-
> ments? Well, no. Did he see Clara Fraser do it? Well, no. [175]

Vickery took the stand in late April. One reporter observed:

> Four phrases dominated his testimony. "Not to my knowledge,"
> "I don't recall," "I haven't the faintest idea" and "I really don't
> know" were his most frequent answers to questions posed by
> lawyers for City Light and for Ms. Fraser.[176]

The hearing finally ended on May 27, and opposing lawyers had a few days to file final briefs.

The ACLU and the National Lawyers Guild filed an amicus brief on Fraser's behalf. In it, ACLU Director Kathleen Taylor emphasized that Fraser's case would affect the free speech of every city employee.

Hearing Examiner Sally Pasette had 20 days to issue her proposed findings and conclusion. On June 20, she ruled that City Light

> discriminated against [Fraser] on the basis of political ideology in removing her as coordinator of the ETT Program and in laying her off. She failed to establish that she was discriminated against on the basis of her sex.[177]

It is ironic that Pasette did not recognize that City Light's hostility to Fraser's outspoken feminism and activism on behalf of women workers constituted sex discrimination.

Pasette's proposed "order for relief" had five directives to the utility:

> 1. Back pay...less interim earnings, unemployment compensation, gifts, loans and expense reimbursements...$54,312
> 2. Compensation...for actual expenses incurred by her as a result of...unfair employment practices...$3,489
> 3. Compensation...for embarrassment, humiliation, and indignity suffered...$300
> 4. Reinstatement...into the position of Education Coordinator [at the] Department of Lighting or such other Department...
> 5. ...$21,185 in attorney's fees and costs incurred[178]

Total out-of-pocket for the city: $79,286. Additionally, the Human Rights Department would monitor City Light's treatment of Fraser for two years, with quarterly reports sent to the department for the next 12 months. Suddenly City Attorney Doug Jewett wished the city had settled for $30,000 in May 1979. In a *Seattle Post-Intelligencer* article the day after Pasette's ruling

> City Attorney Doug Jewett expressed dismay...at what he called the "absurdity" of pursuing a case that pitted one city department against another and at the huge expenses incurred during the course of the legal battle.
>
> "Total cost to the city has been at least $250,000," Jewett said.

The city had a chance to cut its losses, but it didn't, he said, adding that the city "lost more than it should have."[179]

A month after Pasette issued her proposed ruling, the civilian hearings panel overturned it, along with most of her findings and every element of her recommended relief. It was a split vote, with middle-class, white panelists Darlene Allison and Beverly Stanton gutting Pasette's decision, while Elizabeth Ponder, a Black community activist and Republican, supported Pasette's ruling.

The *Seattle Sun*, a community weekly, took time to research the qualifications of the three members of the hearing panel:

> [Darlene] Allison, who is the wife of Seattle attorney John Allison, listed attendance at one meeting of the National Organization for Women, while [Beverly] Stanton claimed no direct involvement in any organization but did indicate a casual acquaintance for 10 years with an unidentified employee of City Light.
>
> Conflicting stories have been told about recruitment of the... panelists Allison and Stanton....
>
> Evonne Banks, former president of the Women's Rights Commission, explained the emphasis in the selection process was not so much upon finding peers as "on finding free and independent thinkers who could make a decision based upon the facts in the hearing."[180]

A *Seattle Post-Intelligencer* article, "Rehiring of Clara Fraser Overturned by City Panel," reported:

> Elizabeth Ponder issued a dissenting opinion that City Light engaged in unfair employment practices against Fraser because of sex and political ideology.[181]

Only Ponder recognized the sexism in City Light's treatment of Fraser. The *Seattle Sun* article included an extensive interview with Ponder, who had been appointed to the hearings panel by the Human Rights Department.

> Ponder, an activist in civil and women's rights and black community affairs....offer[ed] some insights into the six-month-long

hearing process....

"It was too heavy a case for us," Ponder said. "It was like being a first grader in a sixth grade class. I couldn't see overturning [Pasette's] decision. She's a lawyer."[182]

Dona Cloud, City Light's lawyer, told the press, "City Light management is naturally ecstatic" [183] about the reversal.

Fraser was angry *and* analytical.

> I challenge the whole procedure because [panelists Allison and Stanton] don't understand discrimination or the law....
>
> They can only reverse the hearing examiner if they find errors of law. Pasette understands civil liberties law. They [Allison and Stanton] are two non-lawyers who have substituted their opinion for hers and they can't do that.[184]

Fraser's attorney, John Beckwith, stated Fraser could appeal the decision to Superior Court.

The *Seattle Times* ran the story the next day, "Clara Fraser Outraged, Indignant at Panel's Ruling." She was not the only one who was indignant. The assistant director of the Human Rights Department, Joel Salmi, who had investigated Fraser's case, said this was

> the first time he could remember a citizen hearing panel overruling an examiner to find in favor of an agency accused of job discrimination.
>
> ...Salmi, describing himself...as very disappointed, said the Human Rights Department now will review the hearing-tribunal's findings to decide whether it can and should contest the case further. The department may ask the panel to reconsider, and it could appeal to Superior Court.[185]

Almost immediately, the department filed a motion asking the hearing panel to reconsider its ruling. They must have upheld their original decision, because that same week, Fraser's lawyer filed a motion with King County Superior Court:

> [Beckwith's] motion claimed that the [hearing] panel's decision is against the law.

A Sampling of Supporters of Fraser's Case against City Light

AFSCME Locals 2083, 2083-N, 189, Seattle and Portland, OR

AIM for Freedom Defense Committee, Portland, OR

Alaska Cannery Workers, Seattle

Amalgamated Transit Union Local 587, Seattle

Ti-Grace Atkinson, feminist theoretician, NYC

Ramona Bennett, Native American leader, Tacoma, WA

Black Panther Party, Southern California Chapter

Boilermakers Local 104, Seattle

Committee to Defend Iranian Legal Rights, Seattle

Coors Boycott Committee, Seattle

Feminist Women's Health Center, Los Angeles

Dick Gregory, political satirist

Gary Iwamoto, Asian Law Association, Seattle

Jewish Feminist Coalition, Los Angeles

Flo Kennedy, Black feminist attorney, NYC

King County Labor Council, AFL-CIO, Seattle

William Kunstler, constitutional rights attorney, NYC

Lesbians of Color Caucus, Seattle

Live Without Trident, Seattle

Yolanda Martinez, Seattle Women's Commission

Ruth Messinger, City Councilwoman, NYC

He added that the decision constituted an abuse of discretion and is not supported by the evidence. It "jeopardized the rights of all employees to freely express their political opinions," he said.[186]

Fraser's appeal to King County Superior Court came before Judge T. Patrick Corbett who

> gave Fraser the go-ahead for her suit against the city, but rejected her request that the city pay for the legal costs of pursuing the action. He also refused to stick the city with the tab for transcribing some 6,000 pages of testimony from an earlier [the Pasette] administrative hearing held on that matter.[187]

(The city rejected Fraser's offer of a complete, typed draft of the transcript, to be prepared by volunteers, under the direction of her attorney. Corbett insisted Fraser pay for an official transcript, with an estimated cost of $15,000.)

Legal representation on both sides of the case changed when Fraser's case moved to Superior Court. Feminist attorney Valerie Carlson replaced HRD-appointed John Chen Beckwith as Fraser's independent lawyer. Labor activist and socialist Fred Hyde joined Fraser's legal defense team by December 1980. Both Carlson and Hyde were leaders in the Freedom Socialist Party and worked other jobs while representing Fraser on a contingency basis.

Assistant City Attorney Rod Kaseguma stepped in for Dona Cloud to represent City Light, the City of Seattle, and the two hearing panel members who had reversed Pasette's decision.

Elizabeth Ponder, the hearing panelist who supported Fraser's claims, hired her own lawyer because she did not want to provide any support for her opponents on the panel.

Clara Fraser filed a motion asserting her inability to pay legal expenses, which allowed the court to assign public funding to cover these costs. In a November 21, 1980 *Seattle Post-Intelligencer* article, Fraser explained her financial situation.

> Fraser, 57, said she and her son live on the $600 a month she is paid as an editorial and policy consultant for the Freedom Socialist Party.
>
> She said it costs more than that for the two of them to live and she is in debt....
>
> "I have experienced great difficulty in obtaining more lucrative full-time employment because of my age, sex, political ideology and the stigmatization I have suffered as a result of the defamatory accusations made against me by the city attorney and City Light management...."[188]

The ACLU filed an amicus brief on the matter

Kate Millett, author of *Sexual Politics*

MUJER, Seattle

Las Mujeres de Colores de Portland, OR

Multnomah County Labor Council, AFL-CIO

National Association of Social Workers, Oregon Chapter

National Lawyers' Guild, National Executive Committee

National Organization for Women, Seattle

New American Movement, three chapters

Oregon State Labor Council, AFL-CIO

Joanna Russ, science fiction writer

Seattle Gay Community Center

Paul Skyhorse, Native American activist, Los Angeles

Juan Soliz, Legal Center for Immigrants, Chicago

Gloria Steinem, *Ms. Magazine*, NYC

Union of Lesbians and Gay Men, Los Angeles

United Feminist Front, Seattle

United Construction Workers Association, Seattle

Howard Wallace, gay rights pioneer, San Francisco

Leonard Weinglass, civil liberties attorney, Los Angeles

WFSE Locals 1488, 1020, 435, 341, Seattle and Everett

Merle Woo, Asian American Studies lecturer, Berkeley

Workers World Party

Michael Zinzun, Coalition Against Police Abuse, Los Angeles

supporting the assertion that when fundamental constitutional rights like the First Amendment are involved, an indigent civil litigant should not be prevented from appealing an adverse administrative decision because of inability to pay....[189]

All the while, Fraser's list of supporters grew, as did her press coverage, gaining articles in publications including *In These Times* (Chicago), *off our backs* (Washington, D.C.), *What She Wants* (Cleveland), and *The Guardian* (New York City).

By the end of 1980, Judge Corbett had come Fraser's way, telling the city to "get going with the transcript."[190] After more than six months of legal squabbles, Seattle was ordered to pay for the cost of this transcript, with final fiscal responsibility to be decided after the case was settled. When the city finally produced a transcript, Fraser's team had its work cut out:

> Working evenings and weekends, these aides listened to both the city tapes and the Beckwith tapes—poring over the city's garbled, un-proofed transcript, noting obvious departures from the record, correcting misspellings, and inserting omitted passages.
>
> Fraser filed objections to the most misleading passages in July. In August, City Hearing Examiner Pro Tem Sally Pasette, who conducted the 1980 hearing, started the process of certifying the record (to the court). She accepted most of these corrections. At a hearing August 10, she also agreed to include all exhibits offered and refused in the original hearing, to add an explanation that minor errors were left uncorrected as a matter of economy, and to affirm that even though the transcript refers to all women as "Miss," the title "Ms." is the correct one.[191]

As Fraser's appeal inched forward, Mayor Royer's administration faced additional difficulties. By July, five department heads had resigned including Human Resources, Community Development, Office of Women's Rights, Human Rights Department, and the city budget director.[192] In August, Royer asked City Light Superintendent Murray to resign because of his "weak management, serious personnel problems, and faulty communication."[193] (Joseph

Jubliant supporters, including Clara Fraser's son Jon on the left, surround her in the courtroom after her victory is announced by Judge Goodloe.

Recchi, a City Light veteran, became the utility's superintendent in March 1981.)

It took another two years of motions and counter-motions before Fraser's case finally came before King County Superior Court Judge William C. Goodloe, on August 9, 1982.

After allowing both sides to present their opposing views of the case, Goodloe had heard enough. Dispensing with rebuttals, the judge ruled that "the law and the facts" were on the side of Clara Fraser.

> Exultation flooded the courtroom....
>
> Goodloe ordered Fraser reinstated with full back pay and benefits, and the spectators who thronged the courtroom burst into applause and cheers....
>
> Goodloe had some fascinating things to say.
>
> He commended the city's 1979 attempt to settle out of court with Fraser, who, at the time, had agreed to accept what the judge called a "paltry" $30,000 and a job with the HRD. The City

Council's refusal to accept this settlement was, said the judge, "an outrage." (The Council's recalcitrance cost the taxpayers an estimated $250,000 and took another three years out of Fraser's life.)

"It's time to get rid of this thing," the judge declared.

He then exhorted City Light not to be "bigoted and prejudicial," but to treat Fraser "respectfully and honestly." He said he was guided by Harvard psychologist Gordon Allport's *The Nature of Prejudice* in believing that victims of discrimination and oppression reciprocate kindness if that is what they receive.[194]

Not surprisingly, the city hated Judge Goodloe's decision. City Attorney Doug Jewett filed a motion for reconsideration, which was denied by Judge Goodloe.

Whether or not the city would actually appeal Goodloe's decision was the subject of speculation for weeks. Public opinion was on Fraser's side. Two local papers were flooded with letters to the editor supporting the decision. Letters and mailgrams urged the city to

abide by the ruling and to use public money to uphold its Fair Employment Practices Ordinance, not destroy it.

The Washington State and King County Labor Councils passed resolutions supporting the decision and opposing appeal, and urged members to add their individual voices in support of the resolution. The ACLU also wrote Jewett opposing appeal.[195]

On October 21, 1982, Fraser and the city signed a stipulation agreement that covered her updated back pay, restoration of benefits, expenses, and interest. Judge Goodloe accepted it and Fraser was awarded a total of $135,265.14. Her hard-working lawyers, Carlson and Hyde, received attorneys' fees. About a third of Fraser's settlement went for taxes, pension contributions, and social security. Out of the balance, Fraser made generous donations to the organizations that had supported her and mobilized hundreds of hours of volunteer labor.

The Fall 1982 *Freedom Socialist* article celebrating Fraser's victory, "How Sweet It Is," called out key elements of Fraser's eventual victory:

Fraser's victory was chiefly the product of six factors:

• An extremely strong legal case.

• Tough political conviction on the part of Fraser and her closest allies in the Freedom Socialist Party, Radical Women, and the Clara Fraser Defense Committee.

• A well-organized defense committee that publicized the case far and wide, garnered impressive local, national, and international support, and raised a financial war chest to help defray the enormous case expenses.

• Recognition by key sectors of labor, women, minorities, gays, and progressives that this was a test case of free speech in the '80s.

• Meticulous work by attorneys Valerie Carlson and Frederick W. Hyde, Jr. aided by the Seattle chapter of the National Lawyers Guild and dozens of volunteer lawyer-consultants and legal aides.

• A groundswell of determination by public workers around the country to reverse the anti-labor, anti-affirmative-action tide and beat back the city, state, and federal bosses. [196]

On November 17, 1982, Fraser returned to work as training and education coordinator in the Human Resources Division of City Light. In the almost two years she had initially worked there, she had designed and initiated the ETT program for a multi-racial group of women, helped draft an employee bill of rights, and brought discrimination and the right to free speech on the job to the forefront of public consideration. The terms of her settlement from the City of Seattle and City Light, including a job in her former department, vindicated her claims of discrimination, harassment, and retaliation. The agonizing seven years of struggle also affirmed Fraser's position as an indomitable worksite and community leader.

Teri Bach splices a conductor inside a terminal vault, 1983.

Back on the Grid

Some six years before Clara Fraser won her case, the Office of Women's Rights settled the ETTs' discrimination claim and ordered reinstatement of six of the women. Angel Arrasmith, Teri Bach, Megan Cornish, Heidi Durham, Letha Neal, and Jody Olvera came back to work at City Light as helpers in 1976.

Two other ETTs were still working at City Light, Margie (Wakenight) Bellinger and Patty Wong. Bellinger had transferred to an office position before the ETT program had been terminated, although she would eventually come back to a field job as a substation operator. Wong had been hired as lineworker helper when the other ETTs were laid off. By the time the other ETTs returned, she was a supervisor in range repair. Jennifer Gordon had been hired as a helper at the same time as Wong, but quit months later, unable to endure the stress and harassment. Daisy Jones had taken a job as a bus driver when the ETT program was terminated, but before actually being laid off.

The six returning ETTs were rehired as helpers and also had a mandated opportunity to go into one of the utility's apprenticeship programs. But during this period, City Light only offered apprenticeships in overhead (linework), not in construction or underground. Megan Cornish recalls:

> When we won our case, City Light, which had always had lineworker apprenticeships and constructor apprenticeships every year, went "Oh! We're only going to have a line apprenticeship." Because our victory included that anyone who wanted to [could] go into an apprenticeship program; City Light had to take us. So if we wanted to go for being journey-workers we had to do linework. And Clara encouraged us to do it.
>
> ...I think it was several years before they again had a substation constructor apprenticeship. That forced the other women to stay as

helpers, learn on the job, and eventually take Civil Service exams for various journey-level positions.[197]

Linework was (and is) the most grueling and physically dangerous utility work. The difficulty of the work requires intimate trust between "pole partners" and fosters a macho mystique and a culture of hazing new and/or unpopular co-workers. Crew chiefs, historically, had total power over their crews, so a prejudiced chief could wield immense pressure on apprentices and drive them out of the program. In addition, until the use of bucket trucks became routine, lineworkers climbed poles using spikes attached to their boots, called hooks. Apprentices still climb poles in order to know how to do it if the bucket truck fails. Cornish remembered the strength required:

> Linework...takes more upper-body strength. And because you're standing on a pole, you have to do all the work with just your arms and your upper body.[198]

In October 1976, Heidi Durham, Teri Bach, and Megan Cornish decided to take the risk and enter the lineworker apprenticeship. Jody Olvera, Letha Neal, and Angel Arrasmith continued as helpers, and eventually were allowed to pick which of the three job categories they wanted to work in: overhead, underground, or substation construction. Olvera and Arrasmith chose substations; Neal chose underground.

Twenty-three years later, Heidi Durham wrote about the ETTs' reception when they returned to work:

> Shortly after our return to work, our sweet taste of victory turned sour. Management, being the sore losers that they are, were out to make our lives miserable. Their collective male egos had been crushed by a bunch of uppity feminists beating their butts. This we expected, but what did come as a surprise to us, was the fact that the union was no longer in our corner.
>
> There was a reason for their changed attitude towards us. When one reflects on events, always one finds a reason. Shortly after we were fired, the union went out on strike. After a three-month long battle, they went back to work for essentially the same contract

Utility Electrical Work at Seattle City Light
Main job categories and terms in use during the general period of this book

DISTRIBUTION DIVISION
Operates the equipment that feeds electricity to customers, *not* including generation and high-voltage transmission lines.

• **Overhead** Maintains powerlines and equipment on poles. Job titles: crew chief, lineworker, material supplier, line crew helper.* There is one apprenticeship program for linework.

• **Network Underground** Serving high-density commercial areas, it provides networked multiple feeds to each customer to insure reliability. Job titles: crew chief, cable splicer (journey-level), material supplier, helper.*

• **Underground Residential Distribution** Responsible for underground wiring that is fed from overhead power lines to residences and businesses.

GENERATION AND TRANSMISSION
• **Substation Construction** Performs electrical work in substations and powerhouses from secondary wiring to high-voltage equipment. Has its own apprenticeship. Job titles: crew chief, electrician constructor (journey-level), helper.*

• **Substation and Hydro Station Operation** Monitors station equipment, resets relays, operates high-voltage circuit breakers and switches. Switches transmission and distribution equipment on or off as directed by power dispatchers. Senior operators are the journey-level equivalent. Junior operators are in a training category. Hydro station operators run equipment at generating plants.

• **Power Dispatch** Controls the entire electrical system from a central location. Provides switching orders to de-energize equipment, issues work clearances, responds to emergencies. Classified above journey-level. Junior power dispatchers control the distribution system. Senior dispatchers control generation and transmission systems.

METER AND RELAY DIVISION
Meter workers install and repair electrical meters at pay slightly below journey lineworkers. Relay electricians install and maintain protective equipment on high-voltage circuits; paid slightly above journey-level lineworkers.

APPLIANCE REPAIR DIVISION
A service for households and businesses. It had no apprenticeship or journey-level category and has been eliminated.

---

* A helper was an on-ground assistant to journey-workers on their crew. It was the entry-level position for electrical workers and could lead to an apprenticeship. City Light eliminated helpers in the early 1990s. This curtailed opportunities—for women and people of color in particular—to enter electrical trades at a laborer level to gain hands-on experience.

they had walked off the job against. These guys were pissed and demoralized. Pissed at the union leadership, pissed at management and in general pissed at life. They felt betrayed and impotent. So where did they direct their frustrations? At management? No! The union leadership? No! Their frustration was directed at us, because we had beaten the boss when they couldn't.[199]

Each of the six returning ETTs has her own memories of the torment they faced once they returned to work. Several of the former ETTs interviewed remembered the harassment as virtually nonstop during their time as helpers and apprentices.

Megan Cornish remembers she felt "nothing *I* can do will be right,"[200] the same words Jennifer Gordon used to described her solo period of work at City Light months earlier.

Jody Olvera came back to City Light for the same reasons she had originally become an ETT, "I liked the work and I liked the money." She chose to work as a helper in substations because there the pervasive pornography "was at least a little bit hidden."[201] (On a line crew, a woman could expect to ride in a job truck whose interior was plastered with hardcore pornography.)

Kathleen Merrigan, another Radical Women member, was hired as a helper at City Light in 1983 and shared co-housing with Bach for a time. She recounted an incident Bach had endured during this period in which Bach was

> taped up, like tied up, but with [electrical] tape, and stuck in a crew cab and left there.... I think she had to kind of break out of it and hop down. Because they had tied her legs together. And hop on to the dock, where somebody finally let her loose.[202]

Merrigan also recalled that Bach had the attitude "she couldn't give in" even though the linework apprenticeship was so punishing that Bach "would come home and just fall out on her bed and sleep without taking her clothes off."[203]

Jody Olvera recalls her first three months back at City Light as unrelenting "silence. Months of silence, where no one on a crew would talk to me."[204] At one point, a co-worker threw a three-pound hammer at her from across the street, yelling for her to catch it. Luckily, it hit her hand, not her head.

As lineworker apprentices, Megan Cornish, Teri Bach, and Heidi Durham had to learn the perilous and difficult skill of pole-climbing in an actively hostile environment. Cornish recalls that even men who supported the women were afraid to speak out against the harassment because they might then be targeted for similar persecution. And with Fraser gone, the women lacked a sympathetic and available advocate in the Training Department.

Marilyn Bircher, the City Light accountant who played a leadership role in the 1974 walkout, became an informal troubleshooter and on-site advisor. For example, she urged Megan Cornish to talk to union shop stewards and safety personnel when she was pushed to work faster than she was able, and when co-workers were throwing tools down at her from poles rather than lowering them in a canvas bucket as normal.

At 23, Heidi Durham was the youngest of the original ETTs, and she took to linework, earning "satisfactory" to "good" evaluations from her first two crew chiefs in every element except "quantity of work." During her first eight months, several of Durham's Apprenticeship Monthly Rating Reports included comments about her struggling with speed although slowly improving. One problem was not being given enough opportunity to perform the actual work:

> In November [1976] I expressed my concern to Tom Harmon [a lineman on her crew at the time] about not being allowed to climb on the job. I told him I would never be able to learn the work unless I was allowed to do it and learn what duties were required of me. Harmon agreed. I asked him to talk with the foreman about it, but he refused.[205]

Despite this, Durham's five-month evaluation, for February 1977, states:

> Apprentice Durham is showing continued improvement. She and I have discussed this report and we both feel she will continue to improve.[206]

In April, Durham was assigned to a different crew chief, Frank Karabach, whom Daisy Jones had problems with as an ETT. Megan Cornish remembers that Karabach was infamous as a racist and all-around bully, and that his crew had the worst safety record among line crews.

Durham's evaluations suddenly took a turn for the worse. She received an overall rating in May of "not performing satisfactorily in one or more phases of his [sic] training."[207] Durham's account describes the pressure she was under:

> For three months on this crew, I was laughed at, harassed, and ridiculed. It did not matter whether I was doing the job right or wrong. In particular, when I asked questions of the Helpers, I was laughed at and made fun of. Often I was met with dead silence when I asked a question.[208]

In Durham's June evaluation, her crew chief wrote, "For the length of time she has been an apprentice she should have shown more improvement."[209]

The day after this evaluation, July 1, 1977, was the day Durham got hurt. A reporter from the *Seattle Times* told the story:

> Her evaluation said she wasn't working fast enough. She decided to show them.
> The crew was taking down an old streetlight system that day.
> Durham started scaling the power poles fast, one after the other, racing up, then down and then up the next. Suddenly, her foot hit a hard knot in one of the poles. Instead of digging into the wood, her leg bounced. Durham slipped, falling 28 feet to the ground. She landed in a sitting position.
> Her back was broken.[210]

Heidi Durham's injuries were near fatal. Word spread through the utility, but without the usual concern for an injured colleague. Megan Cornish recalled:

> We heard a radio call about a person down and an aid car needed. There weren't cell phones at the time, but they had phones

in the trucks that they could clip onto customers' phone lines and put in a call. The crew chief put in a call and said, "Who fell?" And then he went and told us.... [A lineman] had the nerve to wait until I'd gotten up a pole and said, "I heard your friend fall down, go boom!"

I also later heard he said bitterly to somebody years later, "God, we successfully drove her [Cornish] off the crews and what does she do but go become a power dispatcher!"....

[He] was really hateful, always....

I think it was right after coffee-break that she fell. I think maybe at lunchtime we [Cornish and Bach, both apprentices and members of Radical Women] checked in with Clara and we decided we needed to get to the hospital. I can't remember if it was after work or mid-day. And we also demanded and got that we needed some time off from climbing and working on the crews every day. Which was *politically* a good thing. I'm not so sure it was a good thing work-wise. It's like when somebody falls, going ahead, working up there on the pole right away, is a good way to get over it. They say.[211]

Press coverage immediately after Durham's fall noted that she was *not* using a safety strap (also referred to as a safety belt). In fact, according to the safety report about the accident, she had been wearing her belt until she "stopped at the streetlight [mounted on the power pole] to unbelt to go around it."[212] Megan Cornish would later recall apprentices were directed *not* to use the safety belt while climbing if they wanted to be "real" lineworkers.

While still hospitalized after surgery, and immobilized in a cast, Durham heard about the safety report on her accident, written by IBEW #77 Safety Officer Dan Haw. Rumor had it the report was not good. Durham wondered why she had never been interviewed for this report, the normal procedure.

At the beginning of August, Durham, still in the hospital, talked with #77 Business Manager Warren Adkins about the safety report and received a copy. Haw had concluded that Durham's accident was "just waiting to happen" because she was a poor worker and

Heidi Durham's accident happened eight days before her 24th birthday. Members of her collective household noted the occasion, and Durham's notoriously salty language, in a card illustrated by housemate Su Docekal.

had refused to "listen to good sound advice from journeymen in the trade" to leave the apprenticeship.[213] That same night, Megan Cornish and Teri Bach raised their objections to the report at the local's City Light unit meeting.

There, enough union members agreed Haw's safety report was "unwarranted and unfair"[214] to pass a motion requesting Haw, who was not present, to attend the next meeting to explain his report. The next month, with Durham still hospitalized:

> Haw attended the September [union] meeting and admitted in front of the membership that his report was based on his belief that "women should get out of linework." Several of our linemen co-workers loudly applauded....
>
> Teri and Megan moved that the membership request Haw to withdraw the report and apologize.... Every male member at the meeting except one voted against the motion.[215]

After 13 weeks, Durham was finally released from the hospital at the end of September.

> When I got out, I wore two leg braces, walked with two crutches and was wearing a full body cast.[216]

Harborview Medical Center's description is more graphic:

> [She] is now in a plastic jacket for spinal immobilization. This jacket will be worn until approximately June 1978 [almost a year after the accident]. At present she requires bilateral short leg braces and crutches to walk.[217]

A born fighter, Durham continued to advocate and organize as soon as she was out of the hospital. With help from Megan Cornish and Teri Bach, she circulated an open letter to the members of IBEW #77, asking them to support revision of Haw's accident report, which the local's Executive Board had already approved. At the local's November membership meeting, Lou Walter, a journey-level lineworker, made a motion that Durham's accident report be reconsidered. This was defeated by one vote. A request for a recount was refused. (Lou Walter would continue to be involved with IBEW #77, and as of 2018, is business manager of the local.)

Next, Walter organized a group of lineworkers to go to the Executive Board with Durham, to ask that the report be rescinded. One member of the board told Durham the way to get the report changed was to ask Haw out on a date and exert her "womanly charms." Even her supporters thought this was funny, though Durham was justifiably outraged. Cornish remembers the insulting "joke," but also Walter's help:

> Lou Walter's support for Heidi and organizing of other Linemen to go to the Exec Board in her defense and to try to get the letter removed from the record, was a very daring act at the time, and he deserves credit for it.[218]

In addition to the union's official resistance to helping Durham, City Light management and the city's Personnel Department did their best to block her from being rehired at a job commensurate with her experience. Late in December, the personnel worker handling Durham's industrial claim used her own vehicle to tail Durham and watch her drive a car. The next day, the caseworker wrote a re-hab doctor at Harborview Medical Center to find out when Durham could return to work, implying she was somehow faking her injuries. Her doctor replied:

> I am not surprised she can drive. To see how really disabled Ms. Durham is, she should be observed climbing stairs (which is difficult for her, even with braces and crutches).[219]

With Vickery still in charge, City Light's administration contin-ued to block placing Durham in an appropriate position. As Megan Cornish recalls:

> This didn't happen to men injured on the job, but Heidi was the first woman electrical worker injured on the job. The first battle was to get her back in an electrical trade job. City Light manage-ment wanted to shuffle her off into clerical work![220]

It would take Heidi Durham more than three years to come back to work at the utility. In addition to fighting for continuing in the trades, Durham was trying to find medical assistance to maximize her physical recovery.

> I believe I can improve further. My goal is to *refine* my currently very abnormal gait, because it adversely affects the musculature of my hips, back, and knees.... I am only 25 and given my youth and strength, I'm convinced that my condition can improve.[221]

Meanwhile, the other electrical tradeswomen continued to face daily harassment. Angel Arrasmith remembers that the former ETTs "received crap that we got the jobs just because we were women." Her response was: "I already been through this. I can do the work, once they show me."[222]

Jody Olvera once came out after work and found bullet holes in her windshield. Another day, she was in the back of a truck loading pallets when a co-worker snuck behind the driver's wheel and took off, trying to pitch her off.

Megan Cornish also had memories.

When I was in the apprenticeship, Bill Colberg was the crew chief. And he actually had the...nerve to sit me down and say, "I'm not going to give you an easier time because of your looks!" Who asked for that...!?! He's giving the impression I'm going to be primping on the job.[223]

City Light did hire one woman for electrical work in 1978. Joanne Ward was hired "off the street," as a helper. At age 38 and a poet, she had worked in theater and as a telephone operator, taught oral interpretation and also speed reading. She had been hired as an installer by the telephone company when she was offered a job at City Light. She was also a member of Radical Women and the Freedom Socialist Party, and had participated in the first employee strike at the University of Washington as a member of the Staff Rights Organizing Committee. Choosing to become a helper wasn't hard:

The pay was better. Five dollars an hour versus three. I'd been interested in non-traditional jobs, but at the time there weren't other women in the trades except for the ETTs.[224]

In order to get through probation, she remembers taking a "mum's the word" approach to her own politics and affiliations when she started work at the South Service Center. It took Ward two weeks to spot another tradeswoman, a woman painter.

Jody Olvera remembers City Light sporadically hiring individual women as helpers and perhaps as apprentices, at about the time Joanne Ward came on. Olvera also remembers these "solo hires got picked off one by one" as they faced worksite harassment alone.[225]

While working as a line crew helper, Ward occasionally had the chance during breaks to try climbing poles. She didn't like it. Two months into the job, she ruptured a disc in her back in a workplace injury. During Ward's five-month recovery, Heidi Durham helped her build a case to return to the trades but transfer to substations.[226]

During this same period, Megan Cornish was having her own difficulties as an apprentice lineworker. The pressure and danger only increased after Heidi Durham's accident.

The linemen were pretty much working out of the bucket trucks but they definitely made the apprentices climb and work on the poles.... The truth of the matter was I was never comfortable going up the poles. I don't think I ever would have made it as a lineman because I had—not a terror—but I did have a mild fear of heights. I always tried to overcome it but I didn't enjoy it—especially after Heidi's accident.[227]

Cornish decided to go for other electrical work, even though it would leave Teri Bach as the only female lineworker apprentice.

> When we were apprentices, a power station operator exam was given, which I passed. A few months after Heidi's accident, I was about to get flunked out of the [lineworker] apprenticeship when I was offered a junior operator position (which was equivalent to an apprenticeship), and took it....
>
> [Teri] was the last [woman lineworker apprentice]. I felt like I deserted her when I got out of the apprenticeship.[228]

Power station operators, who start as junior operators and graduate to senior operators, inspect electrical substations, do switching to de-energize and power-up areas where utility work will be done, and are the eyes and ears for power dispatchers during electrical outages.

One benefit of Cornish's transfer was that her experience as a power station operator would allow her to vouch for Heidi Durham's ability to perform that job. By early 1979, Durham had taken the power station operator's exam, but she was told she had not scored well enough to be put on the hiring roster. When she requested formal notice of her test results, she learned she had scored 64 percent, with the needed percentile set at 65 percent.

City Light's employee relations manager almost immediately offered Durham four possible positions, any of which would "transfer [her] laterally or in a downgrade."[229] Three of the jobs were as engineering assistants, the fourth was as an accounting technician. Megan Cornish remembered:

> We were able to stop management from pushing Heidi into a secretarial position both by raising the history of the utility keeping injured workers on in field jobs, and because by that time, I had

Black electricians were a crucial source of support and training for women in the field at City Light. Among the heroes were Ninus "Hoppy" Hopkins (on piano) and Joe Greene (standing), here rousing spirits at an event at Radical Women's headquarters. Tradeswoman Joanne Ward is on the left.

been an Operator, and could say that Heidi was physically capable of doing the job (which management of course disputed).[230]

In April 1979, the Office of Women's Rights intervened on Durham's behalf. It recommended City Light grant service credit for Durham's "disability incurred in line of service,"[231] which would qualify her to become a junior power station operator. OWR further proposed that

> Ms. Durham be given a written offer of the next available power station operator position and that if a position is not presently open, she be temporarily assigned to work in the Safety Division.... [I]n the past, other disabled workers who are male have been assigned to the Safety Division.[232]

City Light queried Durham's doctors to see if she was physically capable of performing the work of a power station operator. It would take months to convince the utility that a single, one-time, pass-fail physical test was inappropriate, since various worksite and tool modifications might be needed. (Durham continued to use crutches and leg braces for the rest of her life, due to partial paralysis and nerve damage from her fall.)

Meanwhile, Teri Bach inched her way toward becoming the first female journey-level lineworker at City Light. Megan Cornish remembered:

> That Teri made it through that apprenticeship is really a big deal.... The fact that she was single-minded enough that she was able to make it through that program was a big deal. I certainly could never have done it. [233]

When lineworker examination results were released on November 27, 1979, Bach scored second of all the applicants.

But the next day, Bach was working on an emergency call-out when she also had a severe accident. A *Seattle Post-Intelligencer* reporter later described what happened:

> She was in a bucket, working on the lines at Cedar Falls during a windstorm, trying to restore power on a pole above the power-house. A tree had tangled in the wires. Bach was cutting it loose with a [chain]saw when the log suddenly spun free and hit her in the back of the head, breaking her neck. [234]

Megan Cornish adds:

> Her crew was called out at night and went way up to Cedar Falls. It was not in the city at all. And they were getting this tree off the line. And because she was the apprentice, she was proving that she could run this situation. And there were only four or five, maybe six people on the crew. And because it was not in the city, there weren't any streetlights. So they couldn't see exactly what was going on. When she cut the tree off the line, it turned out that the poles on either side were higher so that there was a lot of pressure upward on the line. They couldn't tell [that] the tree was on

there. So as soon as she cut it, the tree went flying up into the air and came back down and hit her on the back of the neck. It was not judged to be her fault. Her whole crew said it wasn't her fault, because if anybody had known that it was like that they would have stopped the job.[235]

Bach later told friends she knew she had been seriously injured and that if she moved her head the spinal injury could be devastating. So she and a crew member held her head steady while they rode in the City Light truck to an emergency room.

It would be most of a year before Bach, amazingly, fully recovered and returned to work. During this time, Heidi Durham was finally appointed a junior power station operator. Cornish recalled:

> When she [Durham] passed both the written test and their one-time-only special physical test, they were forced to shut up and bring her back. That whole fight kept her from returning to work I think about a year longer than necessary.[236]

Like Heidi Durham, Teri Bach had to fight to get her job back after her accident. In Bach's case, the goal was to make it back as a journey-level lineworker. Less than eight weeks after her injury, City Light's new superintendent, Robert H. Murray, wrote Bach to express concern about her recovery. Bach wrote back to Murray to clarify her situation:

> The current lineworker hiring register was published...one day prior to my accident. I placed number two (number one is a man who has already been a lineman for three years). Hiring from that register was started immediately, but I have been skipped over. I request that I be hired as a lineworker retroactive to the date of the release of the register.[237]

IBEW #77 also wrote to Superintendent Murray about Bach's case, outlining six "irregularities" in the way the utility handled her accident, as well as its failure to promote her to journey-level lineworker.[238] Within a week, Superintendent Murray wrote to Bach that her "promotion to journey level lineworker will be effective upon

Training manuals from the 1980 Seattle City Light apprenticeship program. (George Hammer archive)

your return to work."[239]

But when Bach went back to City Light on light duty that October, she was told she would not be promoted to lineworker until she was on full duty. When that happened some three months later, her name was no longer on the lineworker registry and she was told then she could not be reinstated until she took a Civil Service exam. City Light made her a *temporary* lineworker as of her return to full duty, but no one could say when the test required of her might next be offered.

Superintendent Murray couldn't intervene because he had resigned the summer before, at Mayor Royer's request.

In the midst of the Catch-22 that kept Teri Bach from permanent lineworker status, Heidi Durham was finally promoted to senior power station operator. By that time, Megan Cornish had been hired as a power dispatcher. Bach would not receive promotion to permanent lineworker until January 1981.

In November 1981, with the urging of other Radical Women who were concerned about her safety, Bach transferred to the Underground Division, where she became the first journeywoman cable splicer.

There was one young lineworker in particular who supported equal opportunity, wanted to make City Light's apprenticeship program more fair and objective, and was in a position to try to do so. George Hammer had also suffered significant injuries as a lineworker. He spent almost two years getting constructive surgery after a 1978 accident that caused severe injuries to his hands. He then had his own fight to regain a skilled job with City Light. Hammer eventually went into the Safety Department, and then became secretary to the apprenticeship committee.

By 1981, Hammer had been assigned to come up with specific recommendations for City Light's apprenticeship program. He knew from experience that lineworker climbing class was "a washout program. Simply a way to get rid of apprentices the journeymen instructors didn't want or like."[240] So Hammer did copious research on training methods used elsewhere. He designed task lists, training schedules, objective evaluation criteria, objective training procedures, and unbiased testing procedures for lineworker apprentices at City Light.

After about a year of work, he delivered his recommendations.

> I developed this program and gave it to Earl Willey, a very senior supervisor. Gave it to him to see what he thought of it. He said it was not worth a pinch of raccoon shit.[241]

One senior member of the apprenticeship committee, Ken Hunich, also made sure the budget that paid for Hammer's time on this project was cut. (Hunich had been a supervisor involved in implementing the original ETT program.)

Hammer went back to work in the field, but only after he took a six-hour customized physical test that included lowering a 180-pound dummy from a power pole. He passed despite his injuries and was then allowed to do streetlight work, and eventually linework.

It took years for City Light to adopt Hammer's work on the apprenticeship program. He recalled:

> It sat on the shelves someplace for years. And then the superintendent called me into his office and asked, "Is this copyrighted?" I said, "No, I did it on company time." So they took that and put Lenny Korslund's name on it, and said we like this program, we're going to start it. So they changed the author and then they liked it.[242]

Heidi Durham on the job at the Power Control Center in a photo published in the 1991 City Light annual report.

Full Circle

After her long-fought, victorious discrimination case, Clara Fraser returned to work at City Light as training and education coordinator on November 17, 1982. She dug in where she'd left off seven-and-one-half years earlier, under a new superintendent, Joe Recchi, a former City Light engineer. (Recchi succeeded Robert Murray, who had been Vickery's successor.)

Teri Bach was back at work as a journey-level lineworker after recovering from her broken neck. Heidi Durham had become a senior substation operator after her broken back. Margie (Wakenight) Bellinger was a junior substation operator. Megan Cornish was a senior power dispatcher. Patty Wong (now married and using the last name Eng) was a manager in Range Repair. Jody Olvera and Angel Arrasmith were journey-level substation constructors. Letha Neal was an underground network helper.

But despite these workplace advances, many things had not changed for the original ETTs, nor for Clara Fraser. All of them continued to face an almost daily dose of retaliation, unequal treatment, and harassment. And although there was less intimidation once these women reached journey-level or were off the field crews, City Light's ongoing administrative tolerance of discrimination and bullying were significant enough that Seattle's Human Rights Department extended its mandatory monitoring period beyond what the ETTs' original settlement required.

Sadly, as of the beginning of 1983, these women were not the only ones there facing vicious worksite incidents. Other City Light electrical workers who were female or of color were targeted as well. Yet however confrontational, and sometimes illegal, working conditions might be, no one expected what happened on January 6, 1983.

John Franklin, acting director of the Human Rights Department (HRD), filed his own discrimination claim on behalf of women in the electrical trades at City Light. As HRD director for less than a year,

Franklin relied on research that had been done under the previous HRD director, Elbert Guillory.

Jody Olvera remembers being at a party in late 1981 or so, and being asked by a friend how things were going at City Light. Her friend, Patrick Haggerty, had reason to be interested. A musician and early gay activist, he worked at HRD as an investigator and supervisor, and had at one time been in the Freedom Socialist Party. (See Haggerty's song, "The Ballad of Clara Fraser," page 112.)

When Olvera told him some of her recent experiences on the job, Haggerty arranged to formally interview her. He then spent months talking to other women and compiling what he remembers as "ongoing, blatant, extensive, on the money, provable in every detail"[243] examples of harassment and discrimination at City Light.

Once the HRD investigation was completed, Director Guillory prepared to file a class action suit against the utility because its rampant abuses had not been altered by numerous previous individual complaints. Guillory, described as flamboyant, abrasive, and controversial, thought a class action suit would force City Light to quit fighting individual claims and start following the law.

But before he could file suit, Guillory was ushered out of city employment in March 1982 after a Seattle Board of Ethics hearing on reported ethical improprieties. Meanwhile Patrick Haggerty left the department due to health issues. Haggerty posits that John Franklin was brought in as the Human Rights Department's acting director on March 30 to find a way to avoid filing a class action suit against City Light while somehow addressing the serious discrimination charges that had come forward.

HRD Director Franklin filed his complaint *to* his own department, which was unprecedented. In it, he charged City Light with seven years of

> unlawful employment practice...due to sex.
>
> The charge covers all women in Respondent's [City Light's] Electrical Helper classifications and Electrical Apprentice classifications. The Respondent is within jurisdiction and is alleged to have discriminated against the identified class of women due to sex with

respect to on-the-job harassment, intimidation, a discriminatory work environment, training, constructive discharges and other terms and conditions of employment.[244]

Franklin filed this case at the beginning of January and went to the press without even notifying the women involved. Records imply Franklin didn't speak directly with any of the women until almost six weeks after he had filed. On February 3, the *Seattle Times* ran a front-page story on the HRD director's complaint under the headline "Sex-Bias Complaints Spark Action Against City Light."

> "I looked at the complaints taken over the last couple of years and interviewed current employees," [Franklin] said. "There appears to be a systemic problem causing them (women) to fail in the [City Light apprenticeship] program. I could not allow that to continue."....
>
> Franklin said his next step is to investigate specific charges and perhaps issue subpoenas. He said he isn't certain how the problem will be resolved, but said it could involve monetary damages and promises by City Light to improve working conditions for women.
>
> "I believe the women working in the electrical-trades area are being discriminated against and deprived of the opportunity to advance and are being harassed daily on the job," Franklin said.[245]

A few days after the complaint went public, City Light took action in its inimitable, bureaucratic fashion. Assistant Superintendent M.J. Macdonald spent much of the first week of February speaking at various employee meetings, including a crew meeting at the South Service Center where he issued not very veiled threats to the crews to shape up. According to Doris Harris, a City Light gardener who was present, Macdonald

> ordered the men in the field to stop discriminating against women and also stated that settlement of the HRD complaint could cost thousands, if not millions, of dollars which would mean loss of jobs in the field.[246]

As word of the HRD director's complaint spread, other City Light employees filed individual complaints and suits. These charged the utility with ongoing racist and sexist practices.

On February 14, 1983, more than 50 individuals—feminists, members of non-City Light unions, and civil rights organizations—held a demonstration outside the City Light administration building, picketing to show support for the HRD director's complaint. The 18 groups organizing and/or endorsing the rally called themselves the Ad Hoc Coalition for Equal Opportunity at City Light.

On the same day as the picket, Nina Firey, a former City Light tradeswoman, filed suit in Superior Court against the City of Seattle, five City Light linemen, and a supervisor. She cited a series of escalating, intentional, and sometimes life-threatening actions by the men named, as well as ongoing verbal and physical abuse. One example:

> On May 27 [1982], Defendant Korslund ordered plaintiff [Firey] to work with hot electrical wires in a manner in violation of the safety code. When plaintiff complained about the willful disregard for her safety to Korslund's supervisor, Defendant Willey, she received a blatantly hostile response and a reprimand for insubordination.[247]

Firey reported she had already filed two complaints with Seattle's HRD without resolution. "Ex-City Light Apprentice Sues for Sex Harassment" was the next day's *Seattle Post-Intelligencer* headline.

> The 28-year-old Firey was the last woman in the lineman's apprentice program. Had she successfully completed it, she would have been the second woman to assume journeyman lineman status for the Seattle utility.[248]

On February 16, 40 women workers at City Light held a press conference in support of the HRD complaint. The group included three of the original ETTs (Teri Bach, Heidi Durham, and Jody Olvera) as well as "gardeners and electrical helpers, journeymen and power station operators, truck drivers and dispatchers."[249] The women described on-the-job harassment:

Karen Meadows recounted finding human feces covering the shower stall in the women's locker room. Jody Olvera told of receiving obscene pamphlets, being set up for electric shocks, and getting hit with a hammer and a chain saw. Heidi Durham fell from a pole and broke her back in 1977 as a result of pressure following an unnecessarily harsh and subjective performance evaluation. The evaluation was part of the anti-woman atmosphere created by management to drive women out of the lineworker apprenticeship program.[250]

Interestingly, the women at the press conference were clear they wanted management-level changes at City Light that would direct workplace change. They did *not* want their co-workers singled out for discipline. Doris Harris, the Black utility groundskeeper who had witnessed Superintendent Macdonald threaten field workers with the HRD claim, spoke:

> As women in the trades, we are opposed to [the HRD] complaint being turned into an excuse to conduct a witch-hunt on the crews. Indeed, *we* will be the victims of any witch-hunt....
>
> Fundamental changes are needed at City Light, and they must be made in the top layers of management *before* conditions can be improved in the field.[251]

Harris presented the women's formal statement. It included a ten-point proposal "to alleviate discrimination at City Light and make affirmative action a reality."[252] (See next page.)

That same week, six weeks after he had filed the claim, HRD Director Franklin finally met with the women his case represented. Other "interested parties" were also present, including Jody Olvera, by now a journey-level substation constructor, and Heidi Durham, now working as a senior power station operator. Durham summarized the meeting in a memo to Clara Fraser:

On the Question of The Original Women Not being Notified of the Complaint:

[Franklin] apologized that he did not inform us when the complaint was filed. He said that the reason he chose not to was

Ten-Point Plan to Fight Discrimination at City Light

Presented Feb. 16, 1983; later adopted by CERCL

1. Create a full-time position of advocate whose exclusive job will be to represent the day-to-day needs and interests of women and minorities, and to troubleshoot and resolve problems caused by and related to race and sex discrimination.

2. Place the Equal Employment Opportunity (EEO) Officer directly under the Superintendent.

3. Establish a permanent Human Relations Council composed of women, minorities and disabled employees from the field and offices.

4. Institute affirmative action and equal opportunity on-the-job training.

5. Upward mobility through promotions and training.

6. Assign a woman with field experience to the Safety Division to focus on job hazards caused by prejudice, discrimination and harassment.

7. Fund and implement extensive and intensive Human Relations training for all management, supervisory and field personnel.

8. Fund a special apprenticeship program advocate for women and minorities.

9. Appoint women and minority representatives to the Electrical Crafts Apprenticeship Committee (ECAC) and the Joint Apprenticeship Training Committee (JATC).

10. Finally, and most importantly, we demand full representation and participation in all negotiations between the Human Rights Department, the Mayor's Office and City Light.

because he was afraid of his action being leaked out and wanted to avoid any attempts by the other powers in the City from stepping-in and not allowing it to be filed. In retrospect, he thought it would have been better to consult us, because the complaint would have been more accurate and more inclusive.[253]

Durham reported most of those present at the meeting concurred that the complaint, filed only on behalf of women helpers and apprentices, was not broad enough. For example, it did not include Jody Olvera or other women who were no longer apprentices. It also excluded men of color. But Franklin made it clear he would *not* amend his complaint to include other job classifications.

He didn't deny that discrimination existed in other classifications, but the main reason he had decided to file the complaint and restrict it to women [helpers and apprentices] in the electrical trades was because that was where the discrimination was the most blatant and life-threatening and also the Dept. (HRD) had the most documentation to back-up their charges.[254]

Not everyone was on board. An open letter was then circulated by 29 female City Light workers, perhaps trying to discount "troublemakers," stating they did *not* experience discrimination at the utility.

> We feel the allegations which have been made against [male workers at City Light] by a few dissident females to be grossly unfair....
>
> Our own experience has been that of equality and fairness.[255]

In response, Megan Cornish, Heidi Durham, Teri Bach, Jody Olvera, Joanne Ward and 13 other IBEW #77 members wrote to Local #77 staffer Mike Kelley and Business Manager Charlie Silvernale. They charged Kelley, the local's representative at City Light, with organizing workers against the HRD director's complaint and helping to generate the letter disputing discrimination.

> [Kelley is] organizing a few sisters to make the incredible claim that since they personally feel they have not been discriminated against, no one at City Light has ever been! Brother Kelley...should recognize that the question is not whether each and every one has been maltreated, but whether *any* have. In this case, it is most.[256]

The letter also indicted Kelley for his "heavy-handed red-baiting" toward supporters of the director's complaint, for his refusal to allow complaint supporters to use IBEW #77's hall for their press conference the week before, and for Kelley's attempts to dissuade them from talking with the press.

Although Kelley had told the women that IBEW #77 "was neither for nor against the [HRD] complaint," the letter noted he *had* spoken out against the complaint at the King County Labor Council and to at least one other union. Kelley had also demonstrated his disregard for those reporting retaliation when he

> refused to listen to Sister [Teri] Bach about the retaliation coming down.... On the North Service Center loading dock he made a public display—in front of management—of turning his back on her.[257]

The letter closed by requesting a written response and a meeting with Kelley and Silvernale. There is no record of IBEW 77's response.

Meanwhile, HRD Acting Director Franklin sent a memo to City

Light Superintendent Recchi outlining Franklin's plan for resolving the complaint. Franklin did this *before* a determination had been issued; he did it even before the investigation was complete. He offered:

1. We [HRD] will suspend investigatory activity until July 1, 1983, pending settlement efforts.

2. This Department will also explore alternative [apprenticeship] programs, including contacting other utilities and agencies to glean information on any successful programs.

3. A working committee should be created to meet regularly to discuss the options being explored. Such committee should include participants from City Light, HRD, Personnel, utility employees (especially the affected class), and the union.[258]

Franklin then incorporated the exact ten-point proposal that had come from complaint supporters at their February 16 press conference.

Franklin's willingness to suspend the investigation for four months effectively gutted the rest of his proposal. City Light tradeswomen (including Bach, Durham, Olvera, and Harris), union representatives, and others immediately met with City Light Superintendent Recchi and Deputy Superintendent Macdonald at the South Service Center. No one from HRD attended. The meeting's agenda covered Franklin's proposal to create a task force, "the ten proposals issued by the supporters of the HRD complaint," and "retaliation by management against supporters of the...[HRD] complaint."[259]

It was immediately clear that the utility's proposed advisory Work Environment Task Force was a sham. The tradeswomen present wanted no part of it because the other deputy superintendent, John Saven, would select all worker-representatives and no one from the Training, Personnel, or Safety divisions, nor from the Equal Employment Opportunity Office, would be appointed.

Superintendent Recchi would not commit to negotiating with the women named in the complaint, negotiations Franklin had used to justify putting HRD investigations on hold. Recchi also made it clear City Light would not consider, let alone adopt, any of the workers' ten proposals. He and Deputy Superintendent Macdonald refused each of the tradeswomen's proposals for a variety of reasons. One cost too much, several were already in planning stages (more or less), those relating to apprenticeship programming were bound by union contracts. (The utility could have agreed to bring these matters forward during contract negotiations.) Recchi further asserted safety issues were *never* a result of discrimination. He did agree to "talk to" the supervisors and crew chiefs who had issued retaliatory verbal and written orders.

Following the meeting, the tradeswomen present sent Deputy Superintendent Macdonald a memo documenting the discussions. In the two weeks it took him to respond, several unions wrote to the utility and/or the city, stating their support for the HRD complaint, including American Federation of State, County, and Municipal Employees #435, International Federation of Professional and Technical Engineers #17, representing City Light engineers and clerical workers,[260] and the Sheet Metal Workers International Association #99.

During those two weeks, Superintendent Joe Recchi also announced the composition of the 15-member Work Environment Task Force. It included Patty (Wong) Eng, the only ETT who was never part of any discrimination complaint.[261]

When Macdonald finally wrote back to the tradeswomen, he stated the utility would take no action to resolve the HRD complaint, at least until City Light's hand-picked Work Environment Task Force had done its work. This meant the only deadline for any action or change relating to the HRD complaint was July 1, the date HRD Acting Director Franklin had set for the agency to resume its investigation.

Macdonald backpedaled on City Light's outright rejection of the tradeswomen's ten proposals, noting they would be given to the task force to consider "along with proposals from other employees." Macdonald asserted that the retaliatory actions discussed in the meeting "were more general than you indicated in your memo and that they were oriented towards productivity on the job" not discrimination.[262]

By April 1983, the HRD had a new director, Marlaina Kiner, a Black attorney who headed the federal Office for Civil Rights in

Seattle in the 1970s and had also directed the Seattle Human Rights Commission. (This commission advises the mayor, city council, Human Rights Department and other city departments on human rights issues.)

Kiner immediately sent a letter to Sheet Metal Workers #99 acknowledging the local's support for the HRD director's complaint, and informing the union that HRD was trying to resolve the director's complaint without further "proceedings."

Seeing the writing on the wall, that the city managers were going to administratively dispose of the matter, supporters of the HRD complaint decided to create an organization to push for an end to discrimination within City Light. On April 24, the Employee Committee for Equal Rights at City Light (CERCL) announced its formation. It included women and men working in all areas of the utility.

Supporters of the director's complaint had spoken at the Seattle Human Rights Commission's monthly meeting on April 4. Almost a month later, Human Rights Commission Chair William Hobson sent his response to the newly formed CERCL. Citing Franklin's negotiated agreement, which "defers further investigation until July 1, 1983," Hobson claimed that everything about the director's complaint was in the hands of the utility.[263] Shortly after this, City Light's task force began to meet, with HRD staff attending only as observers.

CERCL joined forces with another community group, the Light Brigade, to rally the public against discrimination at City Light. (The Seattle-Tacoma Light Brigade was a consumer-based citizens' group that fought against shutting off electricity to low-income families and against taxpayer subsidies of nuclear power.) Together, CERCL and the Light Brigade sponsored a well-publicized community gathering on discrimination at City Light that was held at the Cannery Workers Hall (ILWU Local #37) in Pioneer Square.

More than 200 people attended the May 10, 1983 event. There were speakers from ten unions and two Native American groups, musicians, dramatic readings, and a skit, as well as CERCL and Light Brigade presentations.

> The hall was vibrant with huge bouquets of flowers, vivid signs

and banners proclaiming "Protest Discrimination at City Light" and "Support Women, Minority and Disabled Workers!"[264]

Heidi Durham spoke as a CERCL member. She began by asking the audience:

> How many of you have....noticed in the left corner of your bill a small red and green emblem with the words "Your Seattle City Light" printed beside it. This is how the utility identifies itself....
>
> CERCL believes the time has come to begin making City Light *really* ours—to make it responsive and responsible to the citizens of Seattle who own it.[265]

(Megan Cornish remembers the utility dropped the slogan "Your Seattle City Light" a short time after this.)

Carol Dobyns, leader of the Light Brigade, denounced City Light's negligence toward ratepayers and employees. Clara Fraser laid out the connections between these issues:

> It all comes together in a meeting like this—the labor-management issue, the internal struggle in the unions, the civil rights issue, civil liberties, and politics. If you haven't got civil rights on the job, and free speech when you work for the government, you haven't got any rights.[266]

The rally built morale and consolidated alliances, but on-the-job harassment continued. Weeks later, Letha Neal, a Black helper and one of the original ETTs, was suspended without pay. Her supervisor, Dan Haw, overheard her say "Heil Hitler" in a comeback to a co-worker and incorrectly assumed she was talking about him. (Haw had authored the malicious Local #77 safety report on Heidi Durham's fall.)

> No investigation was carried out before the suspension [of Neal]. Her fellow and sister workers staged a two-hour stop-work protest meeting the next day....[267]

Neal filed a grievance with IBEW #77 and the local initially pursued it. But as time passed, the local let the matter drop. CERCL supporters, including officials of other unions, criticized the local's inaction, calling it out as a traditional AFL-CIO union that was not interested in representing its own members in matters relating to racism and sexism.

> George Starkovich, executive board member of the Washington Federation of State Employees, chastised IBEW bureaucrats for their non-support. "You will have to be more than neutral tomorrow. The bosses are out for all our hides, and the labor movement's best fighters are the women, minorities, and other workers who've been discriminated against."[268]

City Light's Work Environment Task Force released its report just before Memorial Day. Having spent some $27,000 on a consultant, the task force agreed with CERCL "on the nature and depth of the problem" and adopted many of CERCL's ten proposals as findings. But then the committee made only vague recommendations. City Light happily accepted the task force's report without taking any action.

On-the-job retaliation against CERCL members continued. Long-time office worker and CERCL member Gerry (Geraldine) Parks, who worked in the South Line office,

> was suspended for "aggressive behavior" and for refusing to meet with two supervisors without a union representative present. Her supervisor had refused to specify the nature of the meeting beforehand, and Parks rightly feared harassment for her CERCL activities.[269] ·

(Management's refusal to allow a union representative to be present for a disciplinary meeting violated the union contract.) Parks' suspension came after her supervisors told her that "people are pretty opinionated about the women who have challenged City Light" and that her "problems" were caused by "joining the group."[270]

During this tumultuous year, a newly minted Radical Women member, Kathleen Merrigan, joined the City Light tradeswomen. Merrigan grew up in the Midwest with four brothers and was her dad's most willing helper on household projects and maintenance. Her degree in chemistry gave her the basics of electrical theory, so a job in the trades, especially with her activist sisters, became her goal. She was working as a janitor for Seattle Public Library when she was hired as a line crew helper. After passing probation, she became a mainstay of CERCL.

By mid-summer, in addition to the HRD complaint, at least three other major sex discrimination complaints against City Light had been filed with the Human Rights Department. The July 1 deadline for settling the complaint came and went with no apparent administrative acknowledgement or action.

On July 15, AFSCME Local #2083-C (Seattle Public Library Classified Employees) sent a letter to Mayor Royer and Superintendent Recchi, urging them to adopt CERCL's proposals "as beginning solutions to the historic problems of discrimination at City Light." The letter also requested immediate negotiations begin between the Human Rights Department, the Mayor's Office, and "affected employees and their unions" to put an end to discrimination at the utility.[271] Whatever response might have come back from the Mayor's

CERCL's inaugural rally at the Cannery Workers Union Hall, 1983.

Office, there was still no action on the director's complaint.

City Light allowed retaliatory action to continue. At the end of July, eight CERCL members sent a six-page memo to HRD Director Kiner, requesting she

> intervene immediately and order City Light management to cease retaliating against supporters of [the HRD director's] complaint.[272]

The memo itemized specific retaliations taken against each of the signatories in the six months since the HRD complaint had been filed. There is no record of any response from HRD Director Kiner.

Meanwhile Mayor Royer's administration was more interested in weakening the laws applying to non-discrimination practices than in processing actual discrimination claims on file against City Light.

In November, workers at City Light's North and South Service Centers participated in another work stoppage, citing a safety issue, a practice allowed by contract. For more than two hours, some 250 workers refused to work, protesting the suspension of William Colberg, a crew chief with 23 years at City Light. Colberg had been suspended for his

> "lack of response" to harassment and safety complaints brought forward by a female crew member [Cyndy Baker] and for allowing that crew member to disobey his orders.[273]

(This is the same Bill Colberg who told ETT Megan Cornish her looks wouldn't help her on the job.)

Deputy Superintendent Macdonald showed up on site during the walkout and talked with lineworkers he described as "frustrated and confused."[274] Macdonald blamed Colberg for two extremely serious job-site safety violations by two of his crew members. A live wire had been dropped from a pole to within ten feet of where Cyndy Baker was standing, and, in another incident, power was turned on while she was working on a line.

The intentionality of these events, and how much they were caused by sexual harassment under Colberg, were never part of City Light's response, nor did IBEW #77 pursue the matter. (In 1985, the city paid Baker $35,000 to settle a lawsuit over these violations.)

A day after the walkout, Macdonald told the *Post-Intelligencer* Colberg was disciplined because he should have resolved "the deteriorating work situation." Macdonald then suggested Colberg take the "human relations training for all field employees beginning next year."[275]

On December 19, 1983, the HRD issued legal notice that the director's complaint was settled. HRD Director Marlaina Kiner and City Light Superintendent Recchi formally agreed that the Human Rights Department and City Light

> have met in conference and conciliation and desire to settle this matter without further investigation or proceedings.[276]

In theory, any "retaliation or discrimination of any kind" against those supporting or named in the HRD complaint would void this settlement. The HRD would "continuously review compliance" with the settlement for three years, and could void it, and/or start new investigations if it found lack of compliance.[277]

The settlement also explicitly required City Light to comply with Seattle's Fair Employment Practices Ordinance. (The utility's continued flagrant violations of this ten-year-old ordinance had been the basis for many of the discrimination claims against it.) The utility administration was mandated to discipline staff who did not abide by these directives.

City Light was further ordered to start a new co-ed four-year apprenticeship program, beginning in January 1984. It would include up to seven women, and "specifically address…safety issues and problems unique to women in [City Light's] electrical positions."[278]

Any female who made it through this new program and passed "the appropriate City examination" was, like all apprentices, guaranteed a position at City Light. The new apprenticeship program would include monthly evaluations using predetermined standards, to be reviewed by IBEW #77 prior to the start of the program. Scoring these evaluations would be done by a person with "demonstrated ability to work with women and minorities." There would be "reasonable opportunity for all female electrical apprentices to meet regularly with the Apprentice Coordinator to monitor their program and identify potential problems." The settlement also outlined the

Linda Evans was hired as an apprentice lineworker in 1984. She suffered injuries, unequal training, and biased job evaluations. She was fired in 1988 and filed a race and sex discrimination complaint with the Seattle Human Rights Department.

"major human relations training program" for all field employees[279] that Deputy Superintendent Macdonald had mentioned months before, when disciplining William Colberg for allowing discrimination against Cyndy Baker.

The utility was required to implement a redesigned Lineworker Apprentice Climbing School for all line apprentices, one that was better-geared to "those without prior climbing experience," and would "eliminate any bias toward women or minorities." City Light would "try to include at least one woman" in its Safety Unit. And finally, the utility would "provide [the Human Rights Department] with proof of compliance...on a quarterly basis."[280]

By the time the settlement was approved, City Light had submitted its proposal for the new climbing school to IBEW #77, and IBEW had agreed to bring the proposal forward as part of its next contract negotiations with the utility.

City Light had given IBEW #77 most of a month to review and agree to elements of the settlement. CERCL members had about a week. The day after the agreement was signed and announced, Megan Cornish, speaking for CERCL, could only say the agreement had not gone far enough. The *Seattle Post-Intelligencer* summarized the settlement, by saying City Light

> promised to crack down on anyone who discriminates against
> women apprentices. The women have been advised to expect some
> hazing. But there will be quarterly evaluations of all journeymen
> who train apprentices.
>
> If they can tough it out for four years, the utility also guaranteed
> the women permanent jobs.[281]

Two days after the HRD settlement was signed, John Miller offered a tough-talking editorial on KIRO-TV:

> The new City Light–Human Rights [Department] agreement
> may be well intentioned. But I can tell you there's a way to end
> sexual harassment or discrimination against women electrical
> workers that's far faster. That's the Mayor calling in the head of
> City Light and saying, "this is going to stop...and if it doesn't,
> you're not going to be here."
>
> But these days that's not how it works.[282]

(Ironically, Miller, as a Seattle City Council member, had voted against settling Clara Fraser's case before it went to hearing.)

City Light immediately hired five women into its four-year lineworker apprenticeship program, under a new apprenticeship coordinator, Wilma Fountroy. These were the first female line apprentices in the two years since Cyndy Baker's apprenticeship. One of the five quit almost immediately.

Linda Evans was the only Black woman in the new apprenticeship program, and very likely was the first Black woman to be hired as a lineworker apprentice at City Light. As remembered by Evans and co-tradeswoman Kathleen Merrigan, Evans never received adequate training, though the utility opportunistically used her for photos and a human relations film about City Light's commitment to equal opportunity.

"Linda just couldn't win," says Merrigan. "They'd take her off to do photo and video sessions, and then she'd be criticized for missing work."[283] Merrigan recalls that Evans was small in stature and had several serious injuries because she was not trained on how to work safely for her body type.

Evans told a *Seattle Post-Intelligencer* reporter that she passed most of her monthly field work evaluations, but

> attribute[d] low work ratings to the bias of one crew foreman and the lack of written performance standards for line crew trainees.[284]

After failing to advance to journey-level lineworker status, Evans moved to substation electrician training, but again did not receive enough support to pass the exam. She was fired by the utility in 1988 for failing to complete the two apprenticeships. The utility chose not to assign her to lower-level work. She received little support from the union and lost a race and sex discrimination complaint she filed with the Human Rights Department.

The week after the director's complaint was settled, nine CERCL members filed their own complaint with the Human Rights Department, as victims of "political ideology, sex, race and age discrimination, and in retaliation for CERCL's opposition to employment discrimination [and] support of the Director's Complaint...."[285] The CERCL complaint included the charges women in CERCL had outlined in their memo to HRD Director Kiner five months earlier, and added retaliatory action against Teri Bach.

Bach had been disciplined when she turned in minutes from a safety meeting two minutes late. Her supervisor, Dan Haw, then forbade her to go to EEO officers without his permission. This was a blatantly illegal order. (Haw was the supervisor who wrote the safety report on Heidi Durham's accident that blamed her. He would face formal charges of racial discrimination in 1989.) Two more charges of retaliation were added to CERCL's complaint during this period.

Kathleen Merrigan described what it was like to try to have any worksite discussion of harassment or discrimination at the time.

> I remember when it was like...when you said the "D" word—discrimination—they totally freaked out, totally freaked out. I remember being in a safety meeting and saying something like "discrimination is a safety issue."

"Strike that from the minutes!"

And there was a big debate over whether that was going to stay in the minutes or not, whether or not I had the right to have an opinion, and after the meeting the supervisor, Shore, says "if anybody says discrimination, they can expect to come see me in my office." It was that intense! I mean that's scary!.... That was probably about '84. They just didn't get it. They [utility supervisors] were just covering their butts for sure....[286]

In this tense environment, the support of men of color was still essential to the ability of new tradeswomen to learn their jobs. Merrigan later recalled:

You could count on the Black men, who were mostly helpers or material suppliers, to make life easier. They would teach you and show you how to do things. They didn't hate you.[287]

Concurrently with all of this, Clara Fraser was fighting continued harassment within City Light's Training Unit. Some of her job duties were revoked or reassigned, especially aspects of her job that might involve working directly with those outside the Training Unit. It would take most of a year, but after investigation, the HRD would eventually issue recommendations to Fraser's supervisors: Clara Fraser had to be allowed to do her job.

Shortly after the director's complaint was settled, the Human Rights Department moved ahead with a series of proposed changes weakening the very non-discrimination rules it used in processing discrimination complaints. On January 11, CERCL, the National Lawyers Guild, and others offered testimony against weakening these rules:

Dozens of organizations denounced these changes at a January 1984 public hearing called by HRD, and 1,200 individuals signed a petition in opposition.[288]

Director Marlaina Kiner was unfazed and told the press she would go ahead with implementation despite vocal opposition. By the end of February 1984, the HRD had adopted revisions eliminating payment of attorney's fees and punitive damages. The new rules made it impossible for an individual to amend her complaint once it was filed, but allowed the HRD director or the city attorney to amend or withdraw findings and orders after they had been issued.

A coalition of worker, civil rights, and legal groups was created to challenge the rule changes HRD had adopted. Members of the Ad Hoc Committee for Fair Employment and Open Housing included CERCL, Blacks in Government, NAACP, National Lawyers Guild, City Light Black Employees Association (CLBEA), National Conference of Black Lawyers, Stonewall Committee for Lesbian/Gay Rights, the Elder Citizens Coalition, *Seattle Gay News,* Freedom Socialist Party, and Radical Women, as well as

> various unions representing state employees, communications workers, hotel and restaurant workers, and cancer research employees.[289]

The city inadvertently created a stage for CERCL and the Ad Hoc Committee when Mayor Royer suddenly fired City Light Superintendent Recchi on March 30. The *Seattle Post-Intelligencer* ran a detailed account:

> Mayor Charles Royer said yesterday he laid plans as early as last year to ease Seattle City Light Superintendent Joe Recchi out of the top utility post....
>
> "With everybody suing everybody else, the Human Rights Department suing the utility, a big rate increase in front of the [city] council, we just looked awful," Royer said. "We looked like nobody was in charge of the utility."[290]

Royer went on to explain Recchi had been summarily fired because of the way he handled hiring City Light's Customer Services director.

The search was on for a new superintendent. For the rest of the spring, both the Ad Hoc Committee and CERCL watchdogged the selection process. Kathleen Merrigan remembered the renewed urgency of this period of CERCL activism, and the push to take advantage of the opportunities created by the director's complaint.

Ad Hoc Committe for Fair Employment and Open Housing rallies outside the Municipal Building to demand preservation of strong laws for fighting discrimination. Left to right: Heidi Durham, activists Vanessa Gilder and Grace Williams, disability rights fighter name unknown, attorney Fred Hyde, and George Bakan, editor of Seattle Gay News.

It was like [settling] the Human Rights Department complaint wasn't going to do anything unless CERCL got involved and broadened the demands, broadened the whole issue out. That's what made the difference.[291]

In May, Deputy Superintendent Macdonald informed all City Light employees that Gamma Vision, a private human relations consultant, would provide training to all the utility's field workers. There would be two sections, one for all supervisory personnel, and later sessions for the crews. A later issue of *Network*, City Light's employee publication, explained Gamma Vision had been brought in because

a number of formal sexual and racial discrimination complaints have been registered against the utility.... Last Year's Work Environment Task Force put human [relations] training down as one of its priority recommendations. The training is also part of our settlement of the Human Rights Director's Complaint.[292]

In early August, having completed the supervisory portion of the training sessions, Gamma Vision issued a progress report. The consultant stated several times, in several ways, that the large majority of field supervisors (relief crew chiefs, crew chiefs, supervisors, managers, and directors) encountered were "angry, frustrated, confused, misinformed, and unprepared" people who came to the trainings "in a state of resistance, confusion, and sometimes anguish."[293] Gamma Vision summarized "five main observations" from training sessions with supervisory personnel:

1) Employee morale is very low....

2) Employees have little confidence in management....

3) There is resistance to change, specifically to bringing women and minorities into non-traditional jobs....

4) There is confusion among supervisory personnel about job responsibilities and roles....

5) The employees perceive they are not heard by management....

The training team observed more confusion about job roles and responsibilities than anticipated. Many employees perceived their job as "technically getting the job done." The human side of work was not considered an important part of their responsibility as supervisory personnel.[294]

The trainers made 17 recommendations, outlining the need for very specific written policies, definitions, and procedures on disciplinary action, hiring and promotion, and what constitutes discrimination. Consultants further recommended that all supervisory personnel receive training and monitoring in objectively evaluating and communicating employee performance, and that supervisors' own performance evaluations "include measurable human relations skills."[295]

Looking back, Kathleen Merrigan felt the training by Gamma Vision was one thing that did make a difference.

> Gamma Vision did really good training. They talked about language and why isn't "bitchhook" a good name for a tool? And what discrimination is.
>
> And the workforce, they got it. They had cleaner language than I did.... [Gamma Vision] wrote a scathing report that the workforce gets it, management does not. Because management never did. And it all starts at the top. So anything that was going on was condoned by management. But guys on the crews—there was a definite change. And in the union. It went from foreman to crew chief, journeyman to journey-worker. Language was changed. It was just much, much better. And I think partly because a lot of these guys had daughters, had sisters, had wives.[296]

That same August, the Ad Hoc Committee for Fair Employment and Open Housing tried going directly to the city council to get changes. The committee presented a two-page list of proposals to protect the rights of all of Seattle's workers as well as those of City Light's ratepayers.

> Promises of sponsorship and prompt action were given, then withdrawn as Councilwoman Jeanette Williams brought [the proposed amendments] instead before her Operations Committee and the Human Rights Commission for "community input" on August 8.
>
> ...over 20 speakers representing a wide range of groups and interests repeated the January testimony. Three thousand signatures were presented, favoring the amendments, and the Council was accused of foot-dragging.
>
> ...The proposed amendments were sidetracked to yet another Council committee.... [297]

Although the council formed a Human Rights Ordinance Review Panel and held hearings, no action was taken.

Worksite harassment of CERCL and affirmative action advocates continued. Teri Bach, City Light's first journeywoman lineworker, its first journeywoman cable splicer, and avid chair of her work unit's safety committee, was scheduled to be laid off as part of a contrived work reduction by City Light. CERCL rallied to her defense and the layoff was overturned. Bach was transferred to another work location, which prevented her from serving on the safety committee.

Royer's search for a new City Light superintendent continued throughout the summer. In mid-September, he asked the city council to approve appointment of Randy Hardy, which took several sessions. When CERCL members heard Hardy's answers to a number of questions, they put out the call for supporters to ask the council and mayor why Hardy should be hired when, as a *Seattle Post-Intelligencer* article documented:

> Hardy did not hire a single minority person in two-and-a-half years as executive director of the Pacific Northwest Utilities Conference Committee in Portland.[298]

The Seattle City Council unanimously confirmed Randy Hardy as superintendent of City Light at the end of September.

"Radical Socialist Bitches" of IBEW #77

Humor helped the pioneering tradeswomen survive a hostile work environment and gain support from co-workers, even though, as Heidi Durham later recalled, "Mustering up a sense of humor wasn't always easy."

In 1999, Durham recounted an episode from a few years prior, when the feminist tradeswomen heard that Local #77 staffer Mike Kelley was referring to "those of us who were members of Radical Women as Radical Socialist Bitches or RSBs." The women took the offensive and "showed up at the union meeting with buttons on our lapels that said in big, bold letters RSB! In smaller print around the edge of the pin, the acronym was spelled out."

"Our male co-workers, of course, asked what the pins were all about. When we told them that Brother [Kelley] had recently referred to us as RSBs, they said, "Hell, give me one. My wife is an RSB. My daughter is one, too!" By the time the meeting started, several men were wearing the pins and [Kelley] was none too happy! Of course, we were ecstatic!"

In early 1985, CERCL met with Superintendent Hardy. The group wanted him to address issues including backsliding on female representation in the Safety Division and proposed disciplinary measures for employees involved in "vehicular accidents, industrial injuries or near-misses."[299] (Disciplining individuals for safety and/or workplace violations has been shown to be an ineffective way of creating greater workplace safety and compliance; everyone clams up and will not share actual information about the incident.) CERCL also presented examples of continued retaliation against its members and unfair disciplinary action against female and non-white field workers.

Hardy responded that the utility was in the process of addressing many of these matters, that he could not comment on anything relating to CERCL's current Human Rights Department case, and that he had a policy against discussing specific employee "problems." He asserted that City Light would eventually incorporate Gamma Vision's recommendations, which he felt would address many of CERCL's issues. (Gamma Vision's training of non-supervisory field workers was still going on at this time.) CERCL realized not much would change under Hardy's administration.

In addition to challenging utility managers, CERCL also pushed to get IBEW #77 to file grievances on behalf of members who were being discriminated against. Kathleen Merrigan recalled:

> For a long time they [IBEW #77] were just very competitive with CERCL...we [CERCL] had to do all the work for the union. Like we'd write the grievances for women that had problems, like Lois Hairston. I pushed that whole thing [the Hairston issue] all the way through. Which was a big victory for the union....
>
> If there was a situation that was affecting one of the women in the union, [IBEW #77] would say "We can't take your grievance," or "We can't deal with this issue because there's another union brother involved."
>
> But if some woman takes a case to court, then they go, "Well we have to defend our union brother here. It's not that we agree with him."

> I think eventually [the local] got it.... It was a big change for the union....
>
> We always said in CERCL, "We're here because you guys are not doing what you need to be doing. We could disappear if Local #77 would do their job!"[300]

(Lois Hairston, a Black line crew helper, ultimately won her union grievance and a $400,000 discrimination case against the utility for unremitting racist and sexist harassment.[301])

CERCL also tried to get the Human Rights Department to move ahead on the group's complaint, which had been filed almost a year earlier. Megan Cornish requested a status report. The department's response defined its dysfunction:

> As of December, 1984 the majority of cases filed with the [Human Rights] Department have been backlogged, or placed in inactive, pending status.[302]

The letter went on to say that the CERCL complaint *was* moving forward, but very slowly, and that at such time as the department did proceed on the case, it would *not* treat CERCL as a group, but only as individual complainants.

CERCL membership kept growing. It encompassed women and men, tradesworkers and clericals, people of color, immigrants, LGBTQ people, and others.

Doreen McGrath had been following the work of the Ad Hoc Committee for Fair Employment and Open Housing and was a member of Radical Women when she started work in the utility's Information Technology Division. McGrath remembered crossing paths with Clara Fraser and Larry Works, another longtime City Light worker-activist, and that they were "cordial" to each other, but while she was on probation they didn't initially demonstrate their friendship at work. She also got to know and eventually do workplace organizing with Marilyn Bircher (now using her original surname of Robeson), a leader of and spokesperson for City Light clericals during the 1974 walkout, who helped found CERCL. Over 25 years, (Bircher) Robeson had worked her way up to become a cost-accountant and one of the first female managers at City Light. Although in management, she "saw her job as sticking up for, not putting down, her subordinates."[303]

Once McGrath passed probation, she became active in CERCL and helped connect issues of administrative workers with those in trades. She was a major force in the unionization of city information technology workers into International Federation of Professional and Technical Engineers (IFPTE) Local #17 and later IBEW #77. (Other city clerical workers had previously been organized into IFPTE.)

In spring 1986, Clara Fraser retired from City Light. Her worksite accomplishments were many: she'd forced the city to rehire her, won recognition of freedom of speech in the workplace, and mobilized many of her new co-workers into CERCL where they would continue to fight management abuses in the utility's administration building as well as in the field. Fraser told reporters covering her retirement that she was happy to move on to other battles and other organizing campaigns.

Fraser's retirement party was well-attended and memorable for many reasons. Gloria Binns, the longtime CERCL chair, an advocate for Black employees and a customer service representative, presented Fraser with a "Purple Heart" award from the group for "Courage, Tenacity, and Chutzpah." And none other than City Light Superintendent Randy Hardy participated and took the floor to call Fraser the "conscience of the utility."[304]

In August 1986, the Seattle community galvanized after the on-the-job assault of a female lineworker, Sherrie Holmes. An August 29 *Post-Intelligencer* article described Holmes' account of the incident:

> She hung with her arms wrapped around a crossarm while the male line worker tried to yank her loose by her safety strap, until another male worker yelled at the man to stop.[305]

Holmes, two years into her lineworker apprenticeship, was 23 and a Navy veteran. She had been stripping accessories off an old pole. John Harris, a Black journeyman, was using a bucket truck to help lower the old pole's top, after Holmes had cut it off with a chainsaw. Art Myers, a white journey-level lineworker, was about ten feet away on the new pole. He yelled at Holmes not to use the bucket. Holmes quoted Myers as saying she was slow and couldn't do the work, to which Holmes replied she could work a lot slower.

Myers then *walked* on the power lines over to Holmes' pole, an outrageous safety violation. He threatened to punch her, told her to get off the pole, and then attacked her until Harris yelled at Myers to quit. (Harris had started at City Light in 1973, and was one of the earliest African American men to go into the electrical trades.)

Holmes was clear from the beginning that she did not want Myers fired.

> [Holmes] argued that City Light management was to blame for putting female apprentices in "an explosive atmosphere" with some male line workers who resent their presence on this dangerous, physically demanding job.
>
> ...Bill Colberg, supervisor of transmission and distribution, encouraged Holmes to "solve it at the lowest level possible...resolve this at the crew level."
>
> The acting crew chief the day of the incident, Leo Schmitz, said he thought the crew resolved the problem internally after a meeting the next day and decided it was "a personal clash, and that was it."
>
> Holmes reported it to higher authorities....
>
> Holmes said she does not want to be in the middle of a tug-of-war between the utility civil rights groups and the line workers in the field, nor does she want the lineman to become "a martyr" for other linemen.[306]

(Division Supervisor Bill Colberg was the crew chief for the lineworkers who had harassed Cyndy Baker two years before. His suspension as crew chief had caused a City Light walkout.)

Several weeks of investigation ensued while Myers remained on the job. Sherrie Holmes turned to Teri Bach, at the time the only journey-level linewoman at City Light, and an active member of CERCL. (Holmes' co-worker, John Harris, also advised Holmes to contact CERCL.)

As recounted in the *Freedom Socialist:*

Bach received union permission to personally represent Holmes at the hearing on her charges.

Later, a leaflet was issued by the two main civil rights groups at City Light, the Employee Committee for Equal Rights at City Light (CERCL) and the City Light Black Employees Association (CLBEA), demanding quicker action and placing responsibility for the assault on a 12-year management record of social irresponsibility.[307]

Within a month, Superintendent Hardy took action, firing Art Myers and suspending another male lineworker. He then sent a memorandum to all City Light employees about the incident. This worksite travesty colored the public's perception of City Light for years.

In 1987, CERCL took on a new issue that affected everyone working at City Light, a proposed "employee wellness" and drug-testing program that sought to collect significant personal medical information and impose mandatory drug testing. With CERCL educating employees about their rights and IFPTE #17 fighting in court, the wellness program was halted.

The Human Rights Department finally issued proposed findings on CERCL's complaint in late 1989, under its new director, Bill Hilliard. It found "no reasonable cause" for any of CERCL's numerous charges of retaliation. CERCL filed an appeal and had a hearing in February 1993 before the Seattle Human Rights Commission, but the decision was reaffirmed.

CERCL remained active until 1999 as an all-volunteer employee organization, speaking out against management abuses and helping numerous workers, male and female, both in and outside the trades. Working with other employee groups like the City Light Black Employees Association, it fought racial and sexual discrimination, management abuse, retaliation, and harassment at the utility. It also advocated *for* rate-payers and *against* deregulation of the energy industry.

Larry Works, a City Light office worker, CERCL member and former CERCL chair, later described what he had observed and learned working with Durham:

> I've seen Heidi helping people in a number of contexts, especially in CERCL. Over the years, Heidi has encountered a lot of workers at City Light who are suffering. This has to do with our management.... Whenever Heidi encountered a worker who was suffering, whether from discrimination or harassment, there was no hesitation on her part. I think the question she asked of herself, was not should I help but how can I best help. Regardless of who she was dealing with—male or female, whether in the electrical union or elsewhere—there was never a thought of what's in this for me, what can I gain.
>
> Although, she did gain—she gained the reputation of a troublemaker! In helping someone, I never knew Heidi to talk down to [them]. She was flexible and results oriented. If she proposed something and the person didn't want to try that, then she would propose something else. And besides the reputation of a troublemaker, she gained the heartfelt respect and gratitude for her efforts among those who've seen her in action. [308]

Decades of activism and personal commitment by the feminist tradeswomen, other workers at City Light and activists eventually brought a culture-shift to the utility. But issues of racism and sexism are still pervasive at City Light. Between 1995-2017, only seven women of color graduated from apprenticeships into journey-level positions at the utility; in those 22 years, only 38 white women made the grade and 94 men of color. Over the same period, 171 white male apprentices became journeymen.[309]

*   *   *

No one involved with the beginning of the ETT program expected to be immersed in such a morass of politics, personalities, and power. Nor did they foresee that related legal challenges would stretch over decades.

Beginning in 1972, the City of Seattle, under Mayor Wes Uhlman, responded to recent federal affirmative action mandates and passed its own affirmative action ordinances and executive orders (see affirmative action laws appendix). Uhlman also created administrative

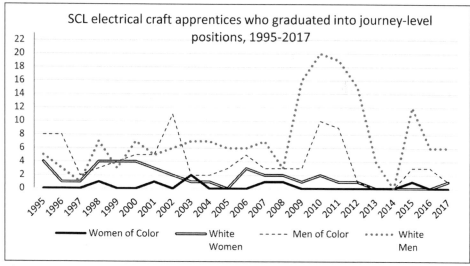

The percent of starting electrical craft apprentices who successfully became journey-level workers at Seattle City Light from 1995–2017: women of color 52%, white women 74%, men of color 74%, white men 84%. Cumulative total hired as journey-level workers over the 22-year period: 7 women of color (2%), 38 white women (12%), 94 men of color (30%), 171 white men (55%).

entities such as the Seattle Women's Commission, the Human Rights Commission, and the Office of Women's Rights. Federal law concurrently required City Light to begin work on a training program for *women* in the field, the ETT program.

Without Seattle's newly adopted legal framework and City Light's need for such a training program, the ETTs and Fraser would never have been hired by the utility. This same combination of new Seattle laws and commissions eventually forced the city and City Light toward real affirmative *actions*, leveraging specific changes neither Uhlman nor Vickery actually supported, as evidenced by Uhlman's unyielding support for Vickery's autocratic sexism and anti-unionism.

If the ETTs had been completely backed by their union from the beginning, their actions would have been more protected, via contract enforcement. (Clara Fraser, as an administrative employee, had no union representation.) When IBEW #77 *did* provide immediate, active support for the ETTs, such as when Vickery issued his "loyalty oath" to the ETTs in late 1974, the utility was forced to limit its hostile response.

Initially, IBEW #77's leadership and many of its members (then virtually all male) were not ready to back the ETTs or the ETT program. Fraser's labor acumen pulled the local in at the program's conception. Her role in getting City Light's non-union workers to join the 1974 electrical workers' walkout set the stage for union representation of the utility's clerical workers a few years later. Once the ETT program was underway, the ETTs, Fraser, and some union members demanded IBEW #77 do its job. And over time, the union did more. Decades after the program had ended, the local formally recognized Bach, Cornish, and Durham's contributions to the union. And over time, IBEW #77 has improved its representation of utility workers on these issues and diversified its staff.

Solidarity among the ten women ETTs has been sometimes overstated, and sometimes under-estimated. The ETTs rarely functioned as a totally unified group. One ETT, Patty (Wong) Eng, claimed never to have experienced *any* level of inequality or on-the-job harassment. At the beginning of the ETT program, several ETTs—Arrasmith,

Gordon, Jones, Neal, Olvera, and (Wakenight) Bellinger—were not seeking anything more, nor less, than to break into an all-male trade. They wanted to pursue a career in this trade both because it paid extremely well and because it required craft expertise.

Three ETTs (Bach, Cornish, and Durham) were members of both the Freedom Socialist Party and Radical Women at the time they were hired by City Light. They came to the ETT program with a strong feminist desire to use their position as trainees to push for equality at City Light. And they each became a worksite leader, inspired in part by Clara Fraser's savvy determination and charismatic leadership.

Once the ETT program started, all of the ETTs (except perhaps Eng) faced an almost daily horror of worksite harassment. Differences in the ETTs' politics did not stop any but Eng from collectively filing their discrimination complaint, less than two months after they started. Over the course of their individual careers at the utility, some spent evenings and weekends preparing legal defenses, rallying supporters, and pushing for press coverage. All contributed by doing their job, day by day. When personal circumstances demanded, some left Seattle City Light.

All of the ETTs, together, made history, forcing a greater degree of equity within City Light, the City of Seattle's administration, the community, and for our future.

Kathleen Merrigan

Nettie Dokes (left) and Janet Greeny demonstrate lineworker skills at the 1992 Women in Trades Fair in Seattle. That year, Dokes became the first Black woman in the country to advance to journey-level lineworker. In 2017, she settled a lawsuit charging City Light with a racist and sexist work environment.

Afterword

By Doreen McGrath

The struggle against gender bias at Seattle City Light didn't end with the last chapter of this book. Other women have carried it forward, but there is still much left to be done.

When I started working at City Light in 1985, energy among the workforce was still high from the Human Rights Department director's complaint and its aftermath. For the next 30 years, I collaborated with CERCL members, fellow unionists, and co-workers to try to hold on to the gains won by the courageous early tradeswomen. We had successes. But in many ways conditions stayed the same.

From my computer job in the administration building, I joined with others to connect the issues of downtown office staff with those of women and people of color in the field. As a tech worker initially in a non-represented position, I twice campaigned with other city "geeks" to organize into a union. First, we joined the International Federation of Professional and Technical Engineers Local #17. But after 15 years, union officials decided they no longer wanted to represent any of the city's information technology personnel! We then joined IBEW Local #77. This would have overjoyed Clara Fraser, who always wanted Local #77 to fulfill the promise of opening its ranks to City Light office staff.

Clara Fraser and the ETTs, especially my sisters in Radical Women and the Freedom Socialist Party, taught many of us how to organize and defend ourselves against management. My co-workers and I continued the fight for workplace equality and fair treatment— a battle that continues to this day.

One legacy of the high-voltage women described in this book is the exceptional frequency with which City Light employees stand up, speak out, and defend their free speech rights on the job.

Many were inspired by the victories of the ETTs and Clara Fraser and by CERCL's demands that sexist, racist and homophobic treatment be stopped. When it didn't, they took action. They filed grievances, EEO complaints, and lawsuits.

Over the past 20 years, many won discrimination cases in court or reached settlements. According to the *Seattle Times,* City Light has paid out over $1.3 million in settlement of discrimination and harassment claims, just in the last ten years.[310] When news of these victories came out, word spread like wildfire among employees. Each one was a vindication for those who experienced similar treatment.

It takes constant vigilance to maintain the right of free speech on the job. We troublemakers made sure to reinforce it whenever we had the chance.

For example, when I crossed paths with my director in the hallway just after learning he was going to lay off five Asian American employees, I stopped him and challenged this action. He dared not retaliate against me even if it really ticked him off because I was well known as a Radical Women member and unionist who knew my rights and could count on widespread support.

The right to free speech also meant my fellow employees could go to a Seattle City Council hearing and testify about financial mismanagement within the utility without fear of reprisal. They could send a letter to the editor defending a wrongly disciplined co-worker and not worry it would trigger retaliation from utility bosses. And if there were repercussions, CERCL and the unions were there to help.

To this day, City Light employees regularly call trusted reporters to blow the whistle on problems at the utility. At city council meetings, on the pages of the newspaper, and on the five o'clock TV news, outspoken employees have held many City Light superintendents accountable and led to more than one being dismissed.

But the patriarchy in the electrical trades has not yet been defeated.

In 1998, Washington voters passed Initiative 200, which outlawed affirmative action. This was a direct hit to the fight for equal opportunity in non-traditional jobs across the state.

Like most employers, City Light immediately dropped its often-inadequate affirmative action plans. As the chart on page 173 shows, the number of women hired into the electrical trades at City Light has stayed scandalously low, with women of color often shut out.

Women continue to sign up for apprenticeships, but few are hired and many don't make it to journey-level because of management's discrimination and lack of commitment to training women for success.

The loss of affirmative action was also a green light to sexual and racial harassment.

Some women hoped to play it safe in this hostile work environment by keeping their heads down and avoiding the pioneering "troublemakers" and "radicals" of the earlier generation of electrical tradeswomen, especially those in CERCL.

Others did complain, protest and demand respect. But utility management continued to cover up and bury complaints, blame the victims, and—if they could—run them off the job.

Women who fought their way to journey-level positions made attempts to improve the apprenticeship programs and in some cases they succeeded. And many women in the apprenticeship office supported the tradeswomen, only to face retaliation themselves. Sounds like the bad old days all over again, doesn't it?

But all is not lost. Experienced fighters such as Alice Lockridge, a retiree from the apprenticeship office, and Kathleen Merrigan, a former cable splicer crew chief, are raising the need for City Light's next Pre-Apprentice Lineworker class to remedy the imbalance by being a racially diverse mix of women only. They call for at least

Some Things *Did* Change

The ETTs dragged IBEW #77 into the modern world.... Union protection eventually limited harassment on-the-job. It held the City Light administration at bay. Things have come a long way.[311]

Larry Works, retired CERCL member

Some of us Black guys sent petitions to the NAACP. We met with [SCL Superintendent] Randy Hardy a couple of times. But we couldn't get to first base. Then things started to change very slowly.[312]

Jerry Lawson, retired SCL crew chief

In linework, they can't just say anymore that that's the one job women can't do. Because there are women there now who are lineworkers and line crew chiefs. Our history has demonstrated that in life.[313]

Teri Bach, former ETT

When I first came on [at SCL] I was a temporary journeyman on an all-male crew. At that time I was identifying as "she." The crew was chill. I got hired as permanent and I worked on a gay crew with a lesbian crew chief. I could see female apprentices who came on got more harassment.

I came out publicly as transgender about a year-and-a-half ago. I had often been mistaken for a guy, and all along I had been treated like one of the guys when we worked. I think that helped.[314]

Aaren Thompson, journey-level electrician constructor at SCL one of the instructors to be female and at least one to be a person of color. Will City Light rise to the challenge? We'll see.

Meanwhile, the globe-shaking #MeToo movement against sexual harassment is making itself felt in City of Seattle employment.

On November 8, 2017, a lengthy article in *The Stranger,* a weekly Seattle newspaper, told the story of how women fighting sexual harassment had met with resounding silence at City Light.[315]

Male supervisors in the high-rise administrative offices were perpetuating a sexually hostile environment in the utility's energy conservation group—patting butts, making suggestive comments and more. In 2017, the women began sharing their stories with each other and circulated a petition to the head of city personnel. They complained to City Light's Human Resources Department. They testified to the Seattle Women's Commission and wrote to city council members. But even with #MeToo exploding around the country, no action was taken.

The *Stranger* story blew the façade off the assumption that all was well at Seattle's power company and in city employment. Radical Women held a public meeting on the issue that drew several of the wronged women and representatives of their union. Everyone agreed it was time to organize. They began collaborating on a #MeToo meeting of city staff.

At the first gathering in December 2017, more than 50 women came forward from offices, the field and different city departments. Women of all races told their stories. Black, Latina, Asian American and immigrant women described mistreatment rife with racism and sexism. Black women from city racial and social justice groups denounced discrimination. Men came to support and stand with their colleagues. Homophobia was addressed. Radical Women's retired tradeswomen, Megan Cornish and Kathleen Merrigan, passed on lessons from their decades at the utility, as did others, including me.

From this dramatic beginning, Seattle Silence Breakers was born—a group dedicated to stopping harassment and discrimination of all kinds in the city of Seattle. Its statement of unity demands

that City leadership act immediately to stop all forms of harassment, intimidation, bullying and discrimination that continue to create a hostile work environment. We demand that leadership require a safe and respectful work environment. Harassment may include unwanted, disrespectful, or inappropriate verbal or physical conduct toward an individual because of race, color, religion, creed, gender, sexual orientation, gender identity, national origin, ancestry, age, disability, health status, marital status, families with children status, veteran status, political ideology, and/or immigration status.[316]

In addition, Silence Breakers vows:

We will not tolerate retaliation against victims and advocates. We will exercise our Free Speech rights on and off the job and we will take vocal and visible actions to spotlight these injustices.[320]

In a short time, this determined group has shaken the foundations of City Hall. We have picketed, petitioned, met with officials, influenced the removal of yet another City Light head, and demanded immediate action. We speak out at hearings, talk to the media and raise our voices at rallies.

One of Seattle Silence Breakers' demands is for a strong, independent Office for Civil Rights for the city. As detailed in

And Others Have Not

When I finally got hired in 1986, everybody in the personnel office cheered because they'd witnessed me trying to get in for three years—until a position approved for affirmative action finally opened up. Even now, it appears there's an imbalance in their hiring practices, because the ratio of white male apprentices hired is significantly higher than that of people of color or women.[317]

Jeff Johnson, Black SCL crew chief

During a recent Pre-Apprentice Line class, guys wanted to wash out the only female. One instructor kept talking about how *hard* tower climbing was going to be and lied that there were only 12 jobs available so two of the PALs should leave the class. She became intimidated and thought she should quit. I spent time with her to remind her: *"You're taller, stronger and younger than me. I made it. You can do it!"* It worked. She stuck it out and is now a journey-level lineworker at City Light. Women need someone during their apprenticeship to cheer them on and give good advice. There need to be women teachers in every class.[318]

Peggy Owens, crew chief and journey-level lineworker at SCL

Driving While Black. I was heading back to the Southend shop in a City Light truck. Police followed me for blocks. They pulled me over. "I see you have expired plates with no tab." This was a City Light truck![319]

Jerry Lawson, retired SCL crew chief

this book, the former Human Rights Department forfeited its ability to fight for aggrieved city residents. In its new incarnation as the Office for Civil Rights, it has become a bureaucratic institution where, one staff member told a Silence Breaker, it's not worth filing a complaint!

"Fight! Struggle! Act! Demand!" were Clara Fraser's parting words to the many colleagues who came together at her City Light retirement party in 1986.

Today, a new generation of women and men are doing just what Clara asked, continuing the pressure for respect and equal treatment on and off the job.

Thank you to Clara and the Electrical Trades Trainees for showing us how to do that!

–October 2018

To People Who Want to Go into the Trades

Jump on the chance. You can really make a difference. You can do wonders for the job, the job will do wonders for you.

Watch your back with the men, and don't take shit; give it back.

Be proud, stand tall. I think about how lucky I was to get in on the ground floor and get it open for other women.[321]

Angel Arrasmith, former ETT

If it hadn't been for the...scores of civil rights activists of all colors and both sexes who fought, struggled and died to make this country a better place, I would never have even thought about working in the occupation I have spent my whole life doing. Recipient and benefactor of affirmative action is a label I wear very proudly, in spite of the right wing's rhetoric today.[322]

Heidi Durham, former ETT

Survival and success essentials for women entering trades:

Skills in dealing with people actively sabotaging your success. A support system of at least three people from different viewpoints to offer a range of ways to deal with problems. A coping plan for days when it's really hard. Job-related fitness and strength. Skills on how to stand up and speak out, document/journal and testify for yourself and others.[323]

Alice Lockridge, SCL apprentice trainer for 25 years, now retired

Appendix I
ETT Close-ups

Angel Arrasmith

When Arrasmith applied to the ETT program she was 30, had some experience in electrical work, and wanted to make the same money male journey-level workers did. An unapologetically out "dyke," Arrasmith was not an activist, but she was a fighter. She joined in the ETT actions at City Light because of unrelenting discrimination and harassment. When rehired after the ETT case victory, she worked as a helper, apparently in the Overhead Division. Arrasmith took the constructor exam and became a journey-level worker. She ended up in the utility's electrical shop, then quit because of drug problems. She has recovered and now lives in the greater Seattle area.

Teri Bach

Bach was the first woman journey-level lineworker at the utility and its first woman journey-level cable splicer. After 1976, she had sole custody of her daughter. Bach's neck was broken in a horrific industrial accident in 1979. She overcame this injury and returned to full work duties. An active member of the FSP and RW, and a cofounder of CERCL, Bach continued to provide counsel and support for her City Light co-workers throughout her career, both by word and example. When she retired in 2004, at the same time as Megan Cornish and Heidi Durham, IBEW #77 awarded them each a plaque that read in part, "A true pioneer on behalf of all women in non-traditional trades." Bach died in 2005 at 61 years of age.

Megan Cornish

Cornish had participated in civil rights and antiwar protests from her college days in the 1960s. As a member of RW and the FSP, she was arrested as part of civil disobedience in support of United Construction Workers Association. After the ETT case victory, Cornish advanced from helper to junior and then senior station operator, and later became the first female junior and then senior power dispatcher. She retired as an outage dispatcher, the highest position in the utility trades. Throughout her career at City Light, including helping establish CERCL, Cornish continued to organize and lead political and legal challenges toward a safer, non-discriminatory workplace. Retiring after 30 years at City Light, Cornish continued her activism and now writes and edits for the *Freedom Socialist* newspaper.

Heidi Durham

Durham was the youngest of four siblings who were all highly involved in the socialist, feminist and LGBTQ movements. She found focus for her aspirations and her incredible determination when she stepped up to become an ETT at City Light. She had a major role in ongoing challenges to the Vickery administration while an ETT. Durham entered the lineworker apprenticeship, but broke her back in a 28-foot fall in 1977. Despite being permanently disabled, she fought to return to work at the utility, and became a junior substation operator, then a senior power dispatcher. An early and longstanding leader in both RW and the FSP, a stalwart of the Ad Hoc Committee for Fair Employment and Open Housing, and a founding member of CERCL, Durham served on the FSP's National Committee for many years. She ran for Seattle City Council as an open socialist in 1991, while working full-time. Durham retired in 2004, and died in 2015 at the age of 62.

(Chai) Jennifer Gordon

Gordon—generally referred to by her last name during her City Light days—was an activist in the Gay Liberation Front, the antiwar movement, and with feminist and women's health issues. She was doing office work when hired as an ETT. She had political differences with FSP and RW, but did join with other ETTs to challenge discrimination and worksite harassment. Gordon was not laid off with the other ETTs because she was a top-scoring participant on the Civil Service proficiency tests. She quit work at City Light before the other ETTs came back, unwilling to undergo extreme worksite harassment as the only feminist field worker, especially once she and her co-workers went out on strike. She went on to become a paralegal. She now lives in California and has adopted the first name Chai.

Daisy Jones (Erhart)

At 36, Jones was the oldest ETT. She had previously set up training programs for Model Cities in the Los Angeles area. Jones was forced to seek other work when the ETTs were notified the program had been terminated, because she needed income as the supporter of five children. She then drove bus for King County Metro, where she became the first female transit supervisor. When other ETTs were rehired, Jones was no longer eligible because she had quit SCL. She later married and went by the last name Erhart.

Letha Neal (Neal-Gray)

Neal learned of the ETT program from a friend who worked at the Police Department. She was interested because she "used to tinker with electricity at home"[324] and wanted a real job with real wages. Neal came back to City Light as a helper after the ETT lawsuit was won. She was the last of the ETT participants to take the exam to reach journey-level status and suffered several workplace injuries. But she eventually became the first and only Black female cable splicer at City Light. She embraced the nickname Cannonball given her by the crews, though it was initially a slur on her skin color and physique, and was renowned for her quick and cutting comebacks to work-site harassment. She married Howard Gray after the period covered in this book and died in 2005 at age 53.

Jody Olvera

Olvera applied to the ETT program after she saw it advertised on an unemployment office flyer. A Chicana activist, former member of International Socialists and a lesbian separatist, Olvera often disagreed with RW and the FSP but she did participate in the ETTs' legal challenge. When she came back to City Light, Olvera began as a helper, choosing to work in substations. Olvera's time as helper allowed her to test into journey-level work in substation construction. She became an electrical safety and health specialist, and retired from the utility after a more-than-three decade career. She now lives in Seattle.

Margie Wakenight (Bellinger)

A farm girl from near Mt. Rainier, Wakenight initially worked at City Light as an office worker. She applied for the ETT position in order to earn more money as a single mother. In March 1975, Wakenight was the first ETT to leave the program when she sensed impending layoffs and transferred to a clerical position in City Light's engineering department. In 1978, she returned to the trades doing intermittent work as a substation operator and later became a permanent, fulltime operator. Now retired and living in rural Washington.

Patty Wong (Eng)

Within weeks of beginning in the ETT program, Patty Wong openly criticized the "militancy" of the program and any solidarity between the ETTs. She was not laid off with the others, and, although she was not party to the ETTs' suit, she received a separate settlement.[325] In 1981, she married and had a daughter. Wong (Eng) became a cable splicer helper, a meter electrician, and eventually a supervisor. She died in 2007, at 59, shortly after retiring from the utility.

Appendix 2

The IBEW Local #77 Strike of 1975-76

Battle lines had already been drawn when the IBEW #77 contract with Seattle City Light came up for negotiation in 1975. From the beginning of his term as superintendent (three years earlier), Vickery had taken on the union, determined to shake up what a city official later called a "patronage-laden caste system of uncivil servants."[326] Vickery continued to be both belligerent to and derisive of City Light workers, blaming IBEW #77 for much of his difficulty in managing the utility.

In April 1974, Vickery summarily suspended two union foremen when they took an extended coffee break on the way back from a job, which violated work rules he had just issued. This triggered the walkout of some 700 IBEW #77 members. (A walkout is also referred to as a wildcat or unauthorized strike because the union didn't call it.) The linemen were quickly joined by approximately 300 City Light office workers. Vickery then claimed he had not yet approved the suspension, and that he *might* negotiate, if everyone came back to work. When Mayor Uhlman backed Vickery, there was an immediate attempt to recall Uhlman, which was thrown out on filing technicalities.

To make matters even messier, IBEW #77 members had voted on their contract with City Light days before the walkout. The local did not tally votes until everyone was back to work, and some records indicate the huge majority of votes rejected the contract proposal.

It seems that IBEW #77's members at City Light then continued working, without a contract, for almost 18 months. Charlie Silvernale, IBEW #77's business representative to City Light at the time, recalled that there was an historic "handshake" deal between both sides that when a contract was agreed upon, its terms would be applied retroactively, back to January 1 of that year. Silvernale, who later became IBEW 77's business manager, also remembered the utility's negotiator, Gene Nelson, had called off negotiations after the walkout, saying things had to "settle out." (Nelson had been a business representative at IBEW #77 in the mid-1950s.)

When negotiations resumed sometime in mid-1975, it was still a bad time to take on City Light. Mayor Uhlman was facing his second recall attempt, and even though IBEW #77 was not officially involved in it, many of its members were part of the campaign.

Uhlman lashed out at the union. "Local #77 won't run the City. You guys can go on strike, I don't care," was an early Uhlman salvo to the union negotiating committee, according to Silvernale.[327] Silvernale relayed this message to IBEW #77's business manager, John Starcevich, who told Silvernale, "Go back and bargain."

The local had additional issues as it went back. The strong contracts it had just signed with other utilities made its members at City Light expect equally good terms. (Similar contracts with different employers are sometimes referred to as "comparables.") And City Light *did* have what Silvernale called a "me too" agreement: a 1951 resolution that City Light would match the average of the union's other utility contracts.

IBEW #77's nine-week strike at another regional utility, Puget Sound Power & Light (PSP&L, now Puget Sound Energy), had just been settled with a retroactive 14 percent increase in pay for *all* of its PSP&L workers, because the wages of every hourly worker at PSP&L were pegged to those of its linemen. Months later, Local #77 negotiated a great COLA (a cost of living adjustment to wages, to compensate for inflation) for its Central Washington Public Utility District members. So, when the City Light contract came up for negotiation, union members there wanted comparables. Instead, the city refused to honor its resolution on the matter.

The union had also taken recent actions that only made City Light less likely to work toward settlement. In its early contract proposals, Local #77 had included 15 requests for changes in the Electrical Trades Trainee program that the ETTs had presented to Vickery, which he categorized as "demands." By the end of September 1975, IBEW #77 had sent City Light a letter challenging Clara Fraser's layoff, the ETT program had been terminated, and both the ETT and Fraser discrimination claims were establishing precedents as they made their way through the city's legal process.

IBEW #77's members voted to strike in September 1975, but they didn't immediately walk. By October, the matter was before federal mediation. City Light formally rescinded its "comparable" resolution. On October 17, 1975, 700 Local #77 members at City Light went out on strike after their offer of binding arbitration was refused.

Jennifer Gordon, one of two ETTs the utility had kept on as helpers, was out on strike when she quit, in late November. The ETT discrimination claim had not yet gone to hearing and she did not think it would succeed. In addition, she faced discrimination even on the picket line, including being left on the street when her striking co-workers went in and out of their cars to warm up between shifts of picketing. Thinking she could quit without much fanfare if she did so during the strike, Gordon left her job and declined "for personal reasons" to discuss her resignation with the press.

In the early morning hours of December 4, 1975, a gasoline tanker truck crashed on the Alaskan Way Viaduct. When its trailer ruptured and burst into flames, six high-voltage cables mounted underneath the viaduct burned through, cutting power to major downtown buildings. Asked to supply emergency crews, the union declined because the outage "did not endanger life." Supervisors then performed union linework to make repairs.

Less than a month later, on January 1, 1976, the George Jackson Brigade destroyed a power station that served the wealthy Laurelhurst neighborhood. (This was one of the Brigade's approximately 20 pipe-bombings, between 1975 and 1978, in the cause of fighting U.S. repression and racism.) City Light supervisors again performed the work of striking electrical workers, and made temporary repairs.

Local #77 was still taking a hard line in its January 1976 report to *The Electrical Worker*, IBEW's national magazine:

> This is only a very brief report of our situation. It would take a book to document all the unfair tactics we have been confronted with and are still facing. They say "You can't beat City Hall." Well, we are going to show them that whoever made that statement didn't know Local 77.[328]

Instead, the IBEW International Office undermined the local's position and told it to go back to work, with or without an improved contract, threatening receivership.

The 98-day City Light strike ended on January 23, 1976, with not a single union demand met.

When the ETTs won their discrimination case and were reinstated as helpers less than six months later, many of IBEW #77's members at City Light were angry at the ETTs for their victory, and bitter about the ETTs' monetary awards when they had not even received comparables in their latest contract. Megan Cornish recalled:

> They went back under the same contract that they had walked out over—a terrible sellout and defeat. It was demoralizing, and affected relations with the women on the crews. Our back pay settlement was widely viewed as a lot of money for not doing anything.[329]

Appendix 3

General Chronology

1963

April 6—J.D. (Dorm) Braman becomes Seattle mayor

April—John M. Nelson appointed Seattle City Light superintendent

June 10—Equal Pay Act (for women) signed into federal law

July 15—Seattle Human Rights Commission created

August 28—Civil rights march on Washington, D.C. draws 200,000 people

November 22—Assassination of President John Kennedy; replaced by Lyndon Johnson

1964

April 26—Formation of Mississippi Freedom Democratic Party to oppose disenfranchisement of Southern Blacks by the dominant, pro-segregation Democratic Party

Summer—Freedom Summer fights to register Black voters in the South

July 2—Civil Rights Act signed into law, prohibiting employment discrimination based on race or sex

1965

February 21—Assassination of Malcolm X

July 2—Equal Employment Opportunity Commission (EEOC) begins operations

August 11–17—Riots in Black community of Watts, California

September 8—Delano, California farmworker strike and grape boycott begins, launching United Farm Workers union; strike ends victoriously in 1970

September 24—President Johnson issues Executive Order 11246, which requires government employers to take "affirmative action" to "hire without regard to race, religion and national origin"

1966

July—Founding of the Freedom Socialist Party (Seattle, Washington)

October 15—Founding of the Black Panther Party (Oakland, California)

1967

April 15—400,000 march against Vietnam War in New York City

July—Riots in Black communities of Newark, New Jersey and Detroit, Michigan

October 13—Federal Executive Order 11375 signed, broadening affirmative action to include gender

November—Founding of Radical Women (Seattle, Washington)

1968

April 4—Assassination of Martin Luther King, Jr.

May—Founding of Seattle Black Panther Party

August 25–29—Antiwar protests and police violence at Democratic Party National Convention in Chicago

November 6—Student strike at San Francisco State University; five-month strike establishes Ethnic Studies and equal access to education for people of color

1969

January 20—Richard Nixon becomes U.S. president

July 27—Stonewall Riot in New York City launches modern gay liberation movement

July 28—Seattle Human Rights Department created

August–September—Central Contractors Association (CCA) actions halt every major, federally funded construction site in Seattle

November 15—500,000-plus march against Vietnam War in Washington, D.C.; largest antiwar protest in U.S. history

November 20—Indians of All Tribes occupies Alcatraz Island; lasts 19 months until forcibly ended by U.S. government

December 1—Wes Uhlman becomes Seattle's youngest mayor and the first Democratic mayor in nearly 30 years·

1970

July 14—First meeting of the United Construction Workers Association (UCWA) in Seattle

September 9–15—U.S. Senate hearings on the Equal Rights Amendment (ERA); two female union officials testify in opposition on grounds of preserving protective labor laws for women

November 3—Washington voters approve referendum legalizing abortion

1971

March 24–April 1—U.S. House of Representatives hearings on the ERA; AFL-CIO legislative director opposes it, claiming it would undermine protective labor legislation for women

1972

March—ERA passes U.S. Senate; it is unable to gain ratification by three-quarters of states within 10-year deadline

May 31—Gordon Vickery hired as City Light superintendent

June—UCWA leads protests and shutdown of Seattle construction sites to demand jobs for people of color

June 17—Break-in at Democratic Party presidential campaign headquarters at Watergate Hotel in Washington, D.C. by agents of Richard Nixon's presidential campaign

August—Formation of the Feminist Coordinating Council (Seattle)

August 25—Mayor Wes Uhlman issues executive order establishing affirmative action program for city employment

September—Founding of Coalition of Black Trade Unionists

November 7—Washington State voters pass the ERA

December 4—Seattle Women's Division created (later redefined as Office of Women's Rights and Seattle Women's Commission)

1973

January 22—Supreme Court legalizes abortion in *Roe v. Wade* case

February 28—American Indian Movement occupies Wounded Knee, South Dakota

April 11—Clara Fraser applies for work at City Light

May 14—Seattle Office of Women's Rights created

May 17—Beginning of nationally televised Senate hearings on Watergate break-in

June 4—Fraser hired as education coordinator at City Light

September—Fraser assigned to coordinate the planning and implementation of the ETT program for women

September 18—Seattle Fair Employment Practices Ordinance passed, specifying employers may not discriminate due to race, sex, marital status or sexual orientation, political ideology, and other factors

October—National AFL-CIO votes to support the ERA

1974

January 2—Carole Coe starts work at City Light as Administrative Services director

February 21—Interviews start for ETT program hiring

March 24—Formation of Coalition of Labor Union Women (CLUW)

April—Vickery issues "Disciplinary Code" for City Light employees

April 4—56 ETT candidates selected for final interviews

April 9–20 —11-day walkout at City Light protesting Vickery regime; Clara Fraser becomes a leading spokesperson for dissident employees

April 15—11,000 signatures presented for recall of Uhlman; ruled invalid by city corporate counsel a month later)

April 20—City Light walkout ends

April 30—First meeting of the Bill of Rights and Responsibilities Committee; Fraser is one of three elected employee representatives

May 6—Public Review Committee begins meeting

June 6—Ten women are selected for ETT program by hiring panel

June 24—ETTs' first day at City Light; Vickery holds press conference touting his commitment to affirmative action and the ETT program

July 3—Vickery and Coe abruptly curtail ETT pre-placement training

July 9—Vickery removes Fraser as ETT coordinator

July 10—ETTs are placed in the field without preparation, clothing or equipment

August 5—ETTs file sex discrimination charge with Seattle's Office of Women's Rights; Clara Fraser files sex and political ideology complaint with Office of Women's Rights and Human Rights Department

August 9—Richard Nixon resigns to avoid impeachment due to Watergate revelations; replaced by Gerald Ford

August 20—Public Review Committee submits report to Mayor Uhlman

September—At the IBEW national convention in Kansas City, a national group is formed to address the near total absence of people of color in IBEW's International Office

November 15—ETTs send Vickery a memo with 15 requests, including reinstatement of their original program and Fraser as coordinator

December 6—Vickery demands ETTs sign a loyalty oath or be terminated

December 6—Teri Bach and Black crew member anonymously accused of "fondling" on the job

1975

January 16–July 1—Seattle firefighters' union leads second recall campaign against Uhlman

March 25—Five percent across-the-board City Light "employee reduction" announced

March 29—Anonymous letter charges Jody Olvera, Teri Bach, Megan Cornish and co-workers with drinking on the job

April 30—Draft City Light Bill of Rights and Responsibilities completed

　　　　—U.S. pulls out of Vietnam, ending the war

May 1—All ETTs take and pass line crew helper test

May 6—ETT discrimination complaint amended to include Olvera, Gordon, and Neal, and additional acts of discrimination and retaliation; Wakenight is dropped from complaint because she has left ETT program

May 13—Fraser's job secretly deleted from the upcoming 1976 budget and replaced with a newly titled position requiring its own Civil Service test

May 28—Letter from Coe to ETTs congratulating them on successfully completing the program by passing the helper exam

June 12—ETTs win 90-day delay of layoff

July 1—Second Uhlman recall election loses

July 8—Vickery denounces and rejects revised Bill of Rights and Responsibilities (violating the agreement that ended the walkout)

July 11—Fraser laid-off without notice, because of a "reduction in force"

July 14—Vickery announces 100-employee reduction of workforce through normal attrition

September 16—Job announcement for Civil Service exam for "Training and Education Coordinator"

September 24—ETTs are terminated

October 17—Strike by IBEW #77 workers begins at City Light

1976
January 23—City Light strike ends after 98 days, the longest public employee strike in Washington history; workers end up with significant losses

April 14—ETT case goes to hearing

July 9—ETTs win sex discrimination case, awarded back pay, damages, reinstatement, and retroactive promotion to electrical helper positions

October—Durham, Bach, and Cornish begin working as lineworker apprentices

1977
January 20—Jimmy Carter becomes U.S. president

May 24—Human Rights Department issues findings in Fraser's favor

July 1—Durham falls from pole and breaks her back

1978
January 1—Charles Royer takes office as Seattle mayor

June 28—Supreme Court decision in Bakke case upholds affirmative action in education but undermines quotas

November 7—Initiative 13, attempting to repeal Seattle employment and housing protections for sexual orientation, is defeated two-to-one

1979
March—Vickery resigns as City Light superintendent to become administra-

tor of the United States Fire Administration in Washington, D.C.

May—Robert Murray appointed head of City Light

June—Mayor Charles Royer proposes conciliation agreement with Fraser providing a $30,000 settlement and a job

July 2—City Council rejects conciliation settlement and orders Fraser's case to hearing

October 14—75,000 people participate in the National March on Washington for Lesbian and Gay Rights in Washington, D.C.; the largest political gathering in support of LGBT rights to date

November 27—Examination results for lineworker position place Bach in second place on hiring roster

November 28—Bach suffers broken neck on the job

1980

1980—Office of Women's Rights is reorganized; its enforcement function is transferred to the Human Rights Department

January 10—Bach writes City Light Superintendent Murray asserting her right to be hired as a lineworker

January 14–May 27—Fraser case argued before Hearing Examiner Pro Tempore Pasette and hearing panel

June 17—Seattle City Council gives the mayor power to hire and fire directors of the Human Rights Department and Human Rights Commission

June 20—Hearing Examiner Pasette enters her proposed decision upholding Fraser's claims of political discrimination

July 21—Hearing panel majority overturns Pasette's decision

August—Fraser appeals to Superior Court

1981

January 20—Ronald Reagan inaugurated as U.S. president

February—Joe Recchi becomes superintendent of City Light

February 9—Bach appointed temp lineworker retroactive to January 14, 1981

August 3—12,000-plus U.S. air traffic controllers go on strike; Reagan fires them all when they refuse to return to work after 48 hours—a huge setback for organized labor

December—Mayor Royer issues Executive Order on Sexual Harassment

1982

January—John Franklin appointed interim Human Rights Department director

August 9—Fraser's case comes before King County Superior Court Judge William C. Goodloe, who issues decision in support of Fraser that same day

November 17—Fraser returns to work as training and education coordinator at City Light

1983

January 6—Human Rights Department Director John Franklin files complaint charging City Light with harassment and discrimination against women helpers and apprentices

February 16—Tradeswomen at City Light hold press conference supporting HRD director's complaint and presenting a ten-point plan

March 3—HRD Director Franklin proposes settlement terms to Superintendent Recchi

March 7—Tradeswomen meet with Superintendent Recchi and IBEW #77

April—Formation of Employee CERCL (Committee for Equal Rights at City Light)

May 10—CERCL and Light Brigade sponsor community rally about discrimination at City Light

October–November—National Lawyers Guild circulates petition to stop proposed changes to administrative rules that will gut enforcement of the Fair Employment Practices Ordinance

December 19—Mayor Royer and newly appointed HRD head Marlaina Kiner settle the HRD director's complaint in exchange for promises that City Light will reform itself

December 29—CERCL files complaint with the HRD, charging retaliation against supporters of the HRD director's complaint

1984

Late February—HRD Director Kiner adopts weakened rules that make it much more difficult to win a discrimination complaint

April 2—Ad Hoc Committee for Fair Employment and Open Housing formed to try to reverse new HRD rules

August—City Light Superintendent Recchi fired by Mayor Royer

September—Randy Hardy becomes the Lighting Department superintendent

1985

September 16—Ad Hoc Committee for Fair Employment and Open Housing pickets Seattle City Council to protest weakened protections against job and housing discrimination

November—HRD Director Kiner resigns

1986

March 18—Fraser retires from City Light

June—Bill Hilliard appointed director of Human Rights Department

June 19—Ad Hoc Committee protests revised anti-discrimination ordinances at rally outside Municipal Building

July 11—Ordinance 112903 allows HRD director to suspend or close a complaint case "for any reason consistent with this chapter"

August 7—Workplace assault on Sherrie Holmes; the resulting furor draws new public scrutiny to sexism at City Light

1987
CERCL and IFPTE Local #17 successfully fight broad and intrusive employee "wellness" and drug-testing program

1989
January 20—George H. Bush becomes U.S. president

December 29—HRD finds "no reasonable cause" for CERCL claims of retaliation

1990
January 1—Norm Rice becomes Seattle's first Black mayor

1991
October—Hardy resigns as City Light superintendent

1992
September—Roberta Palm Bradley becomes first female and first Black superintendent of the Lighting Department

1993
January 20—Bill Clinton becomes U.S. president

February 17—CERCL appears before Seattle's Human Rights Commission to argue against the HRD's rejection of their discrimination complaint

1994
December—Gary Zarker becomes superintendent of Seattle City Light

1995
July 29—President Clinton issues guidelines that severely undermine affirmative action

1996
November 18—Seattle ordinance creates Office for Civil Rights to consolidate and replace Human Rights Department and Office of Women's Rights

1997
November 3—California's Proposition 209 goes into effect: a state ban on all forms of affirmative action

1998

January 1—Paul Schell becomes Seattle mayor

February 24—Death of Clara Fraser, 74 years old

November 8—Passage of I-200, ending affirmative action in Washington State in employment, education, and public contracting

1999

July 31—ETT 25-year anniversary celebration hosted by Radical Women

For a more detailed timeline of events during the period covered in HIGH VOLTAGE WOMEN, *contact Ellie Belew at info@elliebelew.com*

Appendix 4

Timeline of Affirmative Action and Anti-Discrimination Laws

Research on the wide range of local and national laws to address discrimination has been surprisingly difficult. The following is not all-inclusive, but does list legislation relating to the events in this book.

1941

Executive Orders 8802 and 9001 issued by President Roosevelt, required all defense contracts to contain a clause pursuant to which the contractor agreed to refrain from discriminating on the basis of race or national origin.

1943

President Roosevelt extended the scope of *Executive Order 8802* to require all government contracts to contain a nondiscrimination clause.

1953

August 13—*Executive Order 10479* issued by President Eisenhower, established the anti-discrimination Committee on Government Contracts.

1954

September 3—*Executive Order 10557* issued by President Eisenhower, specifically prohibited contractors from discriminating on the basis of race, religion, color, or national origin in employment, upgrading, demotion or transfer.

1961

Executive Order 10925 (related to Executive Order 10479) issued by President Kennedy, required federal contractors to certify they would "take affirmative action to ensure that applicants are employed, and employees are treated during employment, without regard to their race, creed, color, or national origin."[330]

1963

President Kennedy extended *Executive Order 10925* to include federally assisted contractors.

Ordinance 92191, during Seattle Mayor Gordon Clinton's term, created the Seattle Human Rights Commission "to promote equality and understanding among Seattle residents and to study, investigate, and make recommendations regarding discrimination based on race, color, religion, and national origin."[331]

1964

July 2—*Civil Rights Act of 1964* signed by President Johnson. Title VII of this act prohibited employment discrimination on the basis of race, color, religion, national origin, or sex and also made it illegal to retaliate against those who sought relief or assisted others in their exercise of rights secured by the law and created the Equal Employment Opportunity Commission (EEOC). (*Amended four times by 1972.*)

1965

July 2—The federal EEOC began operation (*created by the Civil Rights Act of 1964*).

September 24—*Executive Order 11246* (*related to Executive Orders 10479, 10925*) issued by President Johnson. Set requirements for non-discriminatory practices in hiring and employment by U.S. government contractors, mandated affirmative action plans to increase participation of under-represented racial groups and women. Required documentation of hiring and employment practices upon request.

1968

April 11—President Johnson signed the Civil Rights Act of 1968, banning housing discrimination on basis of race, religion, or national origin

April 19—Seattle City Council, under Seattle Mayor Floyd Miller, unanimously passed *Ordinance 96619* prohibiting discriminatory housing practices.

1972

U.S. Congress passed the *Equal Employment Opportunity Act of 1972* (*amending the 1964 Civil Rights Act*) in a fourth attempt to improve the effectiveness of Title VII of the *1964 Civil Rights Act*. It gave EEOC the authority to sue in federal court and increased the jurisdiction and reach of the agency. Required the U.S. president, rather than the EEOC chairman, to select the agency's general counsel.

January 29—*Ordinance 100642* passed by Seattle City Council, under Mayor Wes Uhlman. It mandated fair employment practices and prohibited employment discrimination by any employer, employment agent or agency, or labor organization due to race, age, sex, color, creed or national origin. The legislation was sponsored by Councilmember Jeanette Williams.

August 25—*Mayor's Executive Order Establishing an Affirmative Action Program* issued by Seattle Mayor Uhlman. Created a *voluntary* affirmative action plan for increasing the number of women and people of color in city employment. In response to this executive order, Seattle's Office of Women's Rights, Human Rights Department, and other city departments set overall municipal affirmative action goals.

November 7—Washington State voters passed the Equal Rights Amendment. It was enacted by legislators in March 1973.

1973

September 18—*Seattle Fair Employment Practices Ordinance 102562 (repealing Ordinance 100642)* passed by the Seattle City Council, under Mayor Uhlman. It widened the prohibition on employer discrimination to include marital status, sexual orientation and political ideology.

1974

June 5—*Ordinance 103422 (amending Ordinance 102562)* passed by the Seattle City Council, under Mayor Uhlman. It prohibited certain discriminatory employment practices; defined offenses with respect to discrimination based on any sensory, mental or physical handicap; and made other revisions to the original ordinance.

December 9—*Ordinance 104095 (further amending Ordinance 102562)* passed by the Seattle City Council, under Mayor Uhlman. It clarified certain procedures for enforcing *Ordinance 102562*, limited the filing period of a discrimination complaint to six months after occurrence, separated which claims would go to the Office of Women's Rights, which to the Human Rights Department, and which to the Department of Human Resources; detailed terms of settlement; required future written rules and procedures for hearings on complaints.

1975

August 4—*Ordinance 104839, Open Housing Ordinance (further amending Ordinance 96619)* passed by the Seattle City Council, under Mayor Uhlman, to include prohibitions against housing discrimination based on sex, marital status, and political ideology.

1976

March 25—*Ordinance 105423 (further amending Ordinance 102562)* passed by the Seattle City Council under Mayor Uhlman, with amendments relating to and prohibiting discriminatory practices with respect to employment.

1977–78

Initiative 13, a Seattle ballot initiative that attempted to repeal city ordinances prohibiting employment and housing discrimination based on sexual orientation, makes its way to the ballot. Defeated two-to-one.

1978

Seattle Mayor Charles Royer required city departments to establish yearly departmental goals, by job category, for hiring women and people of color through an affirmative action plan.

1980

June 17—*Ordinance 109115 (further amending Ordinance 97971)* passed by Seattle City Council under Mayor Royer. It revised the selection procedures for the directors of the Human Rights Department and the Human Rights Commission; mayor given power to hire and fire them.

June 17—*Ordinance 109116 (further amending Ordinance 102562)* passed by Seattle City Council under Mayor Royer. Amended definitions of discriminatory practices with respect to employment. Also defined offenses and prescribed penalties, remedies and enforcement procedures.

1981

December—*Executive Order (Sexual Harassment)* issued by Seattle Mayor Royer.

1983

In the last half of 1983, new Human Rights Director Marlaina Kiner proposed revisions to the HRD rules relating to employment and housing complaints. The new rules narrowed the definition of political ideology discrimination, eliminated payment of attorney's fees, prevented amendment of complaints to include reprisals, allowed the HRD director to dismiss a charge and allowed the HRD director or city attorney to amend or withdraw findings after they were issued.

1984

February 15—*Executive Order* issued by Seattle Mayor Royer that affirmed the right of all citizens to receive city services equally, regardless of race, color, sex, sexual orientation, religion, ancestry, national origin, age, marital status, parental status, political ideology or handicap.

March 6—City Council formalized changes to HRD rules adopted in 1983.

1986

July 11—*Ordinance 112903 (further amending Ordinances 102562, 109116, and 104839)* under Mayor Royer, allowed the director of Seattle's Human Rights Department to suspend or close a complaint case "for any reason consistent with this chapter" and clarified definitions of marital status, political ideology, sexual orientation, and sensory, mental or physical handicaps. It also allowed the complaint to be amended with additional discriminatory acts and/or retaliatory actions.

1994

August 1—*Ordinance 117244* under Seattle Mayor Norm Rice. City council authorized domestic partner registration for both same-sex and opposite-sex couples, enabling them to receive the same city benefits as spouses.

1995

July 29—President Clinton issued *Memorandum on Affirmative Action* that called for elimination of any program that "(a) creates a quota; (b) creates preferences for unqualified individuals; (c) creates reverse discrimination; or (d) continues even after its equal opportunity purposes have been achieved."[332]

1997

November 3—California *Proposition 209* went into effect, after having passed a year earlier. It enacted a state ban on all forms of affirmative action.

1998

November 8—*Initiative 200* passed by Washington voters. It prohibited racial and gender preferences by state and local government via any equal opportunity program that granted preferential treatment in hiring. Incorporated into state law as RCW 49.60.400.

Notes

Unpublished sources can be accessed in the papers of Clara Fraser, Heidi Durham, and George Hammer at the Labor Archives of Washington, University of Washington, Seattle.

A Time for Transformers

1   Clara Fraser, *Revolution, She Wrote* (Seattle: Red Letter Press, 1998), p. 359.

2   John F. Kennedy, "The New Frontier," 1960 Democratic National Convention Nomination Acceptance Address, American Rhetoric Online Speech Bank, http://www.americanrhetoric.com/speeches/jfk1960dnc.htm (accessed 23 May 2018).

3   "Executive Order 10925 Establishing the President's Committee on Equal Employment Opportunity," EEOC 35th Anniversary, https://www.eeoc.gov/eeoc/history/35th/thelaw/eo-10925.html (accessed 23 May 2018).

4   Gloria Martin, *Socialist Feminism: The First Decade, 1966-76,* 2nd ed. (Seattle: Freedom Socialist Publications, 1986), p. 125.

5   Carol Perkins, "Round One Goes to Woman in Fight Against City Light," *Seattle Post-Intelligencer,* 29 June 1980, p. A3.

6   Carey Galernter, "Clara Fraser: A Radical in 'the System,'" *Seattle Times,* 5 July 1980, p. A6.

7   Fraser, *Revolution, She Wrote,* p. 122.

8   Trevor Griffey, "United Construction Workers Association: History," Seattle Civil Rights and Labor History Project, University of Washington, http://depts.washington.edu/civilr/ucwa_history.htm (accessed 23 May 2018).

9   David H. Golland, "The Philadelphia Plan (1967-)," BlackPast.org, http://www.blackpast.org/aah/philadelphia-plan-1967 (accessed 23 May 2018).

10 Anne Frantilla, et al., "Historical Note," Seattle Model Cities Program Records, 1967-1975, http://archiveswest.orbiscascade.org/ark:/80444/xv22921 (accessed 23 May 2018).

11 Griffey, "United Construction Workers Association."

12 Emily Lieb, "Uhlman, Wesley Carl (b. 1935)," HistoryLink.org, http://www.historylink.org/File/7854 (accessed 23 May 2018).

13 Ross Anderson, "The Rebirth of Seattle—Wes Uhlman's Legacy Revisited as Paul Schell Begins Job as City's Mayor," *Seattle Times,* 2 January 1998, http://community.seattletimes.nwsource.com/archive/?date = 19980102 &slug = 2726535 (accessed 23 May 2018).

14   Lieb, "Uhlman."

15   Griffey, "United Construction Workers Association."

16   Howard Gillette, "Philadelphia Plan," Encyclopedia of Greater Philadel-phia, http://philadelphiaencyclopedia.org/archive/philadelphia-plan-2/ (accessed 27 June 2018).

17   Golland, "The Philadelphia Plan."

18   Marc Linder, *Wars of Attrition: Vietnam, the Business Roundtable, and the Decline of Construction Unions* (Iowa City: Fānpìhuà Press, 2000).

19   "Uhlman, Wes," Our Campaigns, https://www.ourcampaigns.com/ CandidateDetail.html?CandidateID = 65463 (accessed 23 May 2018).

20   Lieb, "Uhlman."

21   David Wilma, "John M. Nelson Becomes Superintendent of Seattle City Light on May 4, 1963," HistoryLink.org, http://historylink.org/File/3620 (accessed 23 May 2018).

22   David Wilma, "Gordon Vickery Becomes Superintendent of Seattle City Light on May 31, 1972," HistoryLink.org, http://www.historylink.org/ File/3621 (accessed 23 May 2018).

23   Sam R. Sperry, "Uhlman Names Vickery New City Light Chief," *Seattle Times* (31 May 1972), p. A1.

24   David Wilma, "Managing at Seattle City Light, 1973-1989: An Inter-view with Walt Sickler," HistoryLink.org, http://www.historylink.org/ File/2940 (accessed 23 May 2018).

25   Lieb, "Uhlman."

First Sparks

26   Clara Fraser, cover letter with résumé to Department of Lighting Person-nel Division, 11 April 1973.

27   Debby Lowman, "Dissident Speaks: Leader of City Light Revolt," *Seattle Times,* 23 September 1974, p. D1.

28   Clara Fraser, *Clara Fraser v. City of Seattle,* Transcript of Hearing, Vol. 16, p. 14 (Before the Seattle Human Rights Commission and Seattle Women's Commission).

29   Valerie Carlson, "Facts," first draft of preparatory document for Clara Fraser appeal in case against City Light, 2 March 1982, p. 7.

30   Carlson, "Facts," p. 8.

31   Clara Fraser, "Weekly Activity Report," 25 October 1973.

32   Bill Rheubottom, "Weekly Activity Report," memo to W.M. McNerney, 28 November 1973.

33   Bill Rheubottom, "Weekly Activity Report," memo to Carole Coe, 27 December 1973, p. 2.

34 Clara Fraser, "Minutes of Meeting," memo to participants of meeting on ETT project, 14 January 1974, p. 2, 3. (*Fraser v. City of Seattle*, exhibit #38.)

35 Bill Rheubottom, "Weekly Activity Report—February 7, 1974," memo to Carole Coe, 7 February 1974, p. 1.

Breaking In

36 Gordon Vickery, "Shorthand Class," memo to Carole Coe, 27 February 1974. (*Fraser v. City of Seattle* exhibit #71.)

37 Carole Coe, "Meeting with Gordon Vickery—Mon., March 11, 1974," memo to Training Division File, 13 March 1974, p. 3. (*Fraser v. City of Seattle* exhibit #92.)

38 Jody Olvera, interview #2 by Ellie Belew, 6 April 2017.

39 Angel Arrasmith, interview by Ellie Belew, 27 April 2017.

40 Guerry Hoddersen, *Radical Women in the House of Labor: An Historic Re-Entry* (Seattle: Radical Women Publications, 1974), p. 1.

41 Bill Rheubottom, "Activity Report—Week Ending March 28, 1974," memo to Carole Coe, 28 March 1974.

42 "Chronology for ETT Case, AO-165," preparatory document for *Daisy Jones et. al v. City of Seattle* (March 28, 1974: Memo from Clara Fraser to Members of ETT Committee), p. 4.

43 Ibid.

44 Ibid.

45 Wilma, "Managing at Seattle City Light, 1973–1989."

46 Associated Press, "Seattle Electrical Workers Dispute Men's Suspension," *Daily Chronicle* (Centralia, WA), 10 April 1974, p. 7.

47 Ibid.

48 Marilyn (Bircher) Robeson, remarks at "A Tribute to Seattle's Pioneer Women Electricians," 25th anniversary celebration hosted by Radical Women, 31 July 1999, Seattle, WA.

49 "Chronology for ETT Case" (April 13, 1974: Meeting of Vickery, Rheubottom, O'Sullivan, and Coe), p. 5.

50 (Bircher) Robeson, remarks at "A Tribute to Seattle's Pioneer Women Electricians."

51 Frances Ross, *Clara Fraser v. City of Seattle*, Transcript of Hearing, Vol. 4, p. 143. Steve Church, ibid., p. 158.

52 Marilyn Bircher, *Clara Fraser v. City of Seattle*, Transcript of Hearing, Vol. 3, p. 68.

53 Carlson, "Facts," p. 16. (Full text of the agreement is in *Fraser v. City of*

Seattle exhibit #137A.)

54 "Chronology for ETT Case" (May 3, 1974: Memo from Coe to Whaley), p. 5.

55 "Chronology for ETT Case" (May 3, 1974: Memo from Recchi to Coe), p. 5.

56 "Chronology for ETT Case" (May 6, 1974), p. 6.

57 Bill Rheubottom, "Activities Report—Week Ending May 16, 1974."

58 Carlson, "Facts," p. 21.

59 Ibid.

60 Carole Coe, "Electrical Trades Trainee Positions," memo to Bill Rheubottom (22 May 1974). (*Fraser v. City of Seattle,* exhibit #171.)

61 Bill Rheubottom, "Weekly Activity Report," memo to Carole Coe, 6 June 1974.

62 Carlson, "Facts," p. 24.

63 Carlson, "Facts," p. 25.

64 Earl Willey, "Orientation Electrical Trades Trainees," memo to Gordon Vickery, 21 June 1974. (*Fraser v. City of Seattle,* exhibit #211.)

Affirmative Action Warriors

65 (Bircher) Robeson, remarks at "A Tribute to Seattle's Pioneer Women Electricians."

66 Heidi Durham, *Radical Women in Action—The Case of Seattle City Light 1974–1975* (Seattle: Radical Women Publications, 1975), p. 1.

67 Carlson, "Facts," p. 27.

68 "Transcript of Testimony by Clara Fraser, Education Coordinator, Training Division, June 24, 1974," p. 14.

69 Megan Cornish, interview with Kathleen Merrigan by Guerry Hoddersen and Helen Gilbert, 9 January 2017.

70 Clara Fraser, "Presentation to Public Review Committee," 5 August 1974, p. 2–3.

71 Patricia Wong, "Statement to Public Review Committee," 7 July 1974.

72 Cornish, interview by Hoddersen and Gilbert.

73 Ibid.

74 John Harris, remarks at "A Tribute to Seattle's Pioneer Women Electricians," 25th anniversary celebration hosted by Radical Women, 31 July 1999, Seattle, WA.

75 Jody Olvera, "Into the Fishbowl," *From the Ground Up,* p. 9.

76 Ibid.

77 Angel Arrasmith, *Clara Fraser v. City of Seattle,* Transcript of Hearing,

Vol. 7, p. 80–81.

78   "Vickery Denies He Canceled Programs," *Seattle Times*, 11 July 1974, p. A15.

79   Seattle City Light Employees group, memo to the Eleven Member Review Committee, 11 July 1974.

80   "Chronology for ETT Case," p. 9.

81   Joan Williams, *Clara Fraser v. City of Seattle*, Transcript of Hearing, Vol. 24, p. 7.

82   Carole Coe, "Bill of Rights & Responsibilities Committee vs Regularly Assigned Duties," memo to Bill Rheubottom, 31 July 1974. *(Fraser v. City of Seattle*, exhibit #258.)

Powering Forward

83   *Daisy Jones et al. v. City of Seattle*, Verified Employment Complaint, 5 August 1974.

84   Fraser, "Presentation to Public Review Committee," 5 August 1974, p. 1.

85   Ibid.

86   Ibid., p. 5.

87   Ibid., p. 6.

88   Mike Wyne, "Women Trainees Not Happy with Vickery," *Seattle Times*, 6 August 1974, p. B8.

89   Ibid.

90   "Chronology for ETT Case" (August 6, 1974: Memo from Rheubottom to Coe), p. 11.

91   Bill of Rights and Responsibilities Committee, "Bill of Rights and Responsibilities," 30 April 1975, p. 2–3.

92   Cornish, interview by Hoddersen and Gilbert.

93   Ibid.

94   Ibid.

95   Chai (Jennifer) Gordon, Interview #2 by Ellie Belew, 5 April 2017.

96   Margie Wakenight, interview by Helen Gilbert, 18 December 2017.

97   Heidi Durham, *Radical Women in Action—The Case of Seattle City Light, 1974–1975* (Seattle: Radical Women Publications, 1975), p. 3.

98   Heidi Durham, "Women With Tools: Tribute to Tradeswomen Fighting for Equality," speech presented 8 August 1999, San Francisco, CA, p. 4.

99   Durham, *Radical Women in Action*, p. 3.

100 "Seattle Fair Employment Practices Ordinance," Seattle, WA, Ordinance 102562, Section 4, A (1).

101 "Chronology for ETT Case" (September 16, 1974: Training Committee Minutes), p. 12.

102 Ibid.

103 "Report to the Mayor of Seattle from The Eleven Member Review Committee concerning The City of Seattle Lighting Department," 20 August 1974, p. 14, 15. *(Fraser v. City of Seattle,* exhibit #276-A.)

104 "Minority Report" of Public Review Committee, p. 11. *(Fraser v. City of Seattle,* exhibit #276-A.)

105 Lowman, "Dissident Speaks: Leader of City Light Revolt."

106 Carole Coe, "Electrical Trades Trainees," memo to Bill Rheubottom, 21 October 1974. *(Fraser v. City of Seattle,* exhibit #349.)

107 Megan Cornish, interview with Fred Hyde by Ellie Belew, 16 October 2016.

108 Coe, "Electrical Trades Trainees," memo to Rheubottom.

109 "Chronology for ETT Case" (November 1, 1974: Activity Report from Clara Fraser to Coe), p. 14.

110 Angel Arrasmith, et al., memo to Gordon Vickery from Electrical Trades Trainees, 15 November 1974.

111 Ibid.

112 Ibid.

113 Gordon Vickery, "Your Memorandum Dated November 15, 1974," memo to Heidi Durham, 25 November 1974.

114 Barbara Carter (Women's Rights Department investigator), handwritten notes of conversation with Heidi Durham, 26 November 1974.

115 Carlson, "Facts," p. 56–57.

116 ETT Working Committee, "ETT Program," memo to Gordon Vickery, 2 December 1974. *(Fraser v. City of Seattle,* exhibit #394.)

117 Daisy Jones, *Clara Fraser v. City of Seattle,* Transcript of Hearing, Vol. 5, p. 37–38.

118 Gordon Vickery, "ETT Program," memo to ETTs, 6 December 1974.

119 Ibid.

120 Lee Moriwaki, "Sparks Fly Over Training Program," *Seattle Times,* 8 August 1975, p. B4.

121 Charles Silvernale, IBEW Local #77 Business Representative, letter to ETTs, 10 December 1974.

122 Durham, "Women With Tools," p. 4.

123 K. H. Hunich, "Customer Complaint—Improper Conduct of Four-Person Crew," memo to Julian Whaley, 19 December 1974.

Congratulations, You're Fired

124 David Wilma, "Mayor Wes Uhlman Survives Recall Attempt on July 1, 1975," HistoryLink.org, www.historylink.org/File/3596 (accessed 15 June 2018).

125 Bill Rheubottom, "Line Helper/Apprentice Exam," memo to Electrical Trades Trainees, 15 January 1975.

126 Megan Cornish, interview with Fred Hyde by Ellie Belew, 2 August 2016.

127 Eugene Moen and Rebecca Baker, "Post-Hearing Brief of Office of Women's Rights," in *Daisy Jones, et al. v. City of Seattle Department of Lighting*, AO-165 (undated), p. 17.

128 Department of Lighting, "Electrical Trades Trainee Program for Women Fact Sheet," 21 June 1974, p. 3.

129 Al Ottele, "Disciplinary Suspension," memo to Teri Bach, 14 April 1975.

130 Susan Magee, "Re: Daisy Jones v. Seattle City Light Case No. AO-165," letter to Gordon Vickery, 15 April 1975.

131 "Chronology for ETT Case" (April 15, 1975: Report on meeting of Union, Teri, and Mr. Ottele), p. 18.

132 Megan Cornish, notes to first draft of this book.

133 Carole Coe, letter to Charles Silvernale, 29 April 1975, p. 2.

134 *Daisy Jones et al. v. Seattle City Light*, Case No. AO-165, Amended Verified Employment Complaint, 6 May 1975.

135 Heidi Durham, letter to Charles Silvernale, 8 May 1975.

136 Carole Coe, "Electrical Trades Trainee Program," memo to Angel Arrasmith, et al., 28 May 1975.

137 Public Service Careers Program and City of Seattle Personnel Office, "Proposal for the Employment and Training of Electrical Trades Trainees in the Seattle Lighting Department," 8 August 1973, p. 7.

138 Department of Lighting, "Electrical Trades Trainee Program for Women: Fact Sheet," 21 June 1974, p. 1.

139 "Chronology for ETT Case" (June 4, 1975: Letter from Coe to Carter), p. 20.

140 "Chronology for ETT Case" (June 11, 1975: Trainees meet with Starcevich and Silvernale), p. 20.

141 "Chronology for ETT Case" (June 13, 1975: Memo from Daisy Jones to Line Crew Foreman, Karabach), p. 21.

142 Carlson, "Facts," p. 70.

143 Gordon Vickery, "Budgetary Reductions," memo to all employees, 14 July 1975. (*Fraser v. City of Seattle*, exhibit #558.)

144 Chai (Jennifer) Gordon, interview #2 by Ellie Belew, 5 April 2017.

145 Lee Moriwaki, "Sparks Fly Over Training Program," *Seattle Times*, 8 August 1975, p. B4.

146 Ibid.

147 Ibid.

148 Ibid.

149 Barbara Carter, "Determination and Offer to Conciliate," to Gordon Vickery, September 1975, p. 29.

150 Gordon Vickery, letter to Susan Magee, 10 September 1975.

151 "City Light ETTs' Press Release," p. 3.

152 Lee Moriwaki, "Vickery Blasts Sex-Bias Charge," *Seattle Times*, 11 September 1975, p. A11.

153 "City Light Sex Bias Charges Discussed," *Seattle Post-Intelligencer*, 18 September 1975, p. A3.

154 Gordon Vickery, letter to terminated Electrical Trades Trainees, 23 September 1975.

155 Gordon Vickery, "Salary in Lieu of Formal Notice of Termination," memo to terminated ETTs, 23 September 1975.

156 Cornish, interview by Hoddersen and Gilbert.

157 John Hendrickson, "Proposed Decision of the Hearing Examiner for the City of Seattle," *Daisy Jones, et al. v. City of Seattle Department of Lighting*, Case No. AO-165, p. 1.

158 "Decision of the Hearing Panel for the City of Seattle," *Daisy Jones, et al. v. City of Seattle Department of Lighting*, Case No. AO-165, p. 5.

159 Ed Rader, "Women Electricians Win Stunning Victory," *Freedom Socialist*, Spring 1977, http://socialism.com/fs-article/women-electricians-win-stunning-victory/ (accessed 19 June 2018).

160 Lee Moriwaki, "Women Win Back Pay from City Light," *Seattle Times*, 9 July 1976, p. A6.

161 Rader, "Women Electricians Win Stunning Victory."

The People v. Seattle City Light

162 Clara Fraser, "A Socialist on Trial," *Freedom Socialist*, Spring 1980, http://socialism.com/fs-article/a-socialist-on-trial/ (accessed 19 June 2018).

163 Clara Fraser, "Verified Employment Complaint," HRD Case No. A-E-2 (063), OWR Case No. AO-164, 5 August 1974.

164 Joel Salmi, "Determination and Offer to Conciliate," *Clara Fraser v. City of Seattle*, Case No. A-E-2(063), 24 May 1977, p. 2–7.

165 Vivian Caver, "Finding that Settlement Was Attempted and Failed," Case A-E-2 (063), 9 August 1977.

166 Charles Royer, "Clara Fraser Case," memo to Gordon Vickery and Vivian Caver, 7 June 1978, p. 1.

167 Ibid.

168 Ibid., p. 1–2.

169 Frank Chesley, "Royer, Charles (b. 1939)," HistoryLink.org, http://www.historylink.org/File/8265 (accessed 19 June 2018).

170 David Wilma, "Robert Murray Becomes Superintendent of Seattle City Light on May 21, 1979," HistoryLink.org, http://www.historylink.org/File/3625 (accessed 19 June 2018).

171 Carolyn Hall, "Discrimination Charge Aired, Years Later," *Seattle Sun*, 16 January 1980, p. 6.

172 Susan Gilmore, "Fireworks Expected in Bias-Suit Hearing," *Seattle Times*, 18 January 1980, p. A14.

173 Willene Guillory, *Clara Fraser v. City of Seattle*, Transcript of Hearing, Vol. 2, p. 20.

174 Hall, "Discrimination Charge Aired, Years Later."

175 Don McGaffin, TV Editorial, KING-TV, Seattle, 27 February 1980, reprinted in *The Story of Clara Fraser vs. Seattle City Light* (Seattle: Clara Fraser Defense Committee, 1981).

176 P.J. Rader, "Vickery: Clara Fraser Lacked Ability," *Seattle Times*, 25 April 1980, p. D6.

177 Sally Pasette, "Proposed Decision of the Hearing Examiner for the City of Seattle to the Hearing Panel," File No. A-E (063), p. 1.

178 Ibid., p. 14–15.

179 Don Tewkesbury, "Rehire Fraser, City Light Ordered," *Seattle Post-Intelligencer*, 21 July 1980, p. A1.

180 Georgia McFarland, "Fraser Reversed: Why?" *Seattle Sun*, 30 July 1980, p. 5.

181 Don Tewkesbury, "Rehiring of Clara Fraser Overturned by City Panel," *Seattle Post-Intelligencer*, 22 July 1980, p. A11.

182 McFarland, "Fraser Reversed: Why?"

183 Tewkesbury, "Rehiring of Clara Fraser Overturned by City Panel."

184 Ibid.

185 Richard Zahler, "Clara Fraser Outraged, Indignant at Panel's Ruling," *Seattle Times*, 22 July 1980, p. A9.

186 "Clara Fraser Goes to Court," *Seattle Post-Intelligencer*, 25 July 1980, p. D12.

187 Jack Hopkins, "Judge Rules Activist Can Fight On—At Her Own Expense," *Seattle Post-Intellegencer*, 24 September 1980, p. A2.

188 Jack Hopkins, "Fraser Wants Court to Help Pay the Bills," *Seattle Post-Intelligencer*, 21 November 1980, p. A5.

189 "ACLU to the Rescue: Clara Fraser," *ACLU-WA News*, Vol. 12, No. 6, Nov./Dec. 1980.

190 "Quick Transcript Ordered for Clara Fraser," *Seattle Times*, 19 December 1980, p. B3.

191 Janet Sutherland, "Clara Fraser vs. Seattle City Light: Victory in the Transcript Wars and On to Court," *Freedom Socialist*, Fall 1981, http://socialism.com/fs-article/clara-fraser-vs-seattle-city-light-victory-in-the-transcript-wars-and-on-to-court/ (accessed 20 June 2018).

192 Susan Gilmore, "Dudley to Quit City Post, Enter Ministry," *Seattle Times*, 10 July 1980, p. B1.

193 Jane Cartwright, "City Light Head Quits, By Request," *Seattle Times*, 23 August 1980, p. A1.

194 Janet Sutherland, "How Sweet It Is," *Freedom Socialist*, Fall 1982, http://socialism.com/fs-article/how-sweet-it-is/ (accessed 20 June 2018).

195 Ibid.

196 Ibid.

197 Cornish, interview by Hoddersen and Gilbert.

Back on the Grid

198 Megan Cornish, "Sparks Fly at Seattle City Light," workshop presentation at Labor and Working Class History Association Conference, Seattle, 25 June 2017, https://www.youtube.com/watch?v=3AqKdnHdlOY&t=5s (accessed 20 June 2018).

199 Heidi Durham, "Women With Tools," p. 4–5.

200 Cornish, interview with Hyde, 16 October 2016.

201 Jody Olvera, interview #1 by Ellie Belew, 17 February 2017.

202 Kathleen Merrigan, interview with Megan Cornish by Guerry Hoddersen and Helen Gilbert, 9 January 2017.

203 Ibid.

204 Jody Olvera, interview #2 by Ellie Belew, 6 April 2017.

205 Heidi Durham, "Documentation: Harassment on the Job," document listing incidents from October 1976–August 1977, p. 1–2.

206 Earl Willey, note on "Apprentice Monthly Rating Report," February 1977.

207 "Apprentice Monthly Rating Report" for Heidi Durham for the month of May 1977.

208 Durham, "Documentation: Harassment on the Job," p. 4–5.

209 "Apprentice Monthly Rating Report" for Heidi Durham for the month of

June 1977.

210 Kathy Mulady, "After 30 Years, These Seattle City Light Pioneers Are Retiring," *Seattle Post-Intelligencer,* 4 August 2004, p. A8.

211 Cornish, interview by Hoddersen and Gilbert.

212 Dan Haw, "Heidi Durham's accident," memo to Sam Hadley, Executive Board Local #77, 1 July 1977.

213 Ibid.

214 Durham, "Documentation: Harassment on the Job," p. 9.

215 Ibid., p. 10.

216 Heidi Durham, "Statement to Joint House & Senate Select Committee on Workman's Compensation, 7 January 1980, p. 1.

217 Patrick Radecki, M.D., letter to Elaine Bernhoft, Industrial Insurance Desk, 29 December 1977.

218 Megan Cornish, notes to first draft of this book.

219 Radecki, letter to Elaine Bernhoft.

220 Cornish, notes to first draft.

221 Heidi Durham, letter to Dr. Dwight Frost, 6 December 1978, p. 2–3.

222 Angel Arrasmith, interview by Ellie Belew, 27 April 2017.

223 Cornish, interview by Hoddersen and Gilbert.

224 Joanne Ward, interview by Ellie Belew, 27 January 2017.

225 Olvera, interview #2 by Belew, 6 April 2017.

226 Ward, interview by Belew, and written notes 11 November 2018.

227 Cornish, interview by Hoddersen and Gilbert.

228 Ibid.

229 Ken Gorohoff, letter to Heidi Durham, 27 February 1979.

230 Cornish, notes to first draft.

231 Cara Peters, "Placement of Ms. Heidi Durham with the Lighting Department," memo to Ken Gorohoff, 9 April 1979, p. 2.

232 Ibid., p. 3.

233 Cornish, interview by Hoddersen and Gilbert.

234 Mulady, "After 30 Years, These Seattle City Light Pioneers Are Retiring."

235 Cornish, interview by Hoddersen and Gilbert.

236 Cornish, notes on first draft.

237 Teri Bach, letter to City Light Superintendent Robert Murray, 20 January 1980.

238 Patrick Powers, IBEW #77 Business Representative, letter to Robert Mur-

ray, 23 January 1980.

239 Robert Murray, letter to Teri Bach, 28 January 1980.

240 George Hammer, interview by Ellie Belew, 16 August 2016.

241 George Hammer, remarks at "A Tribute to Seattle's Pioneer Women Electricians," 25th anniversary celebration hosted by Radical Women, 31 July 1999, Seattle, WA.

242 Ibid.

Full Circle

243 Patrick Haggerty, interview by Ellie Belew, 4 April 2017.

244 John Franklin, "Director's Employment Complaint," *Seattle Human Rights Department v. City of Seattle, City Light,* Case No. SHR82CE029, 6 January 1983, p. 1.

245 Susan Gilmore,"Sex-Bias Complaints Spark Action Against City Light," *Seattle Times,* 3 February 1983, p. A1.

246 Doris Harris, "Statement to the Media," 16 February 1983, p. 3.

247 Jean Schiedler-Brown, "Complaint in Employment Discrimination and Intentional Torts," in *Nina Firey v. City of Seattle, et. al.,* No. 83-2-02050-6, 14 February 1983, p. 8.

248 Susan Goldberg, "Ex-City Light Apprentice Sues for Sex Harassment," *Seattle Post-Intelligencer,* 15 February 1983, p. C1.

249 Susan Gilmore, "Harassed Women Talk About City Light," *Seattle Times,* 17 February 1983, p. B1.

250 Sandy Welsted, "CERCL Zeroes In on Management Abuses at Seattle City Light," *Freedom Socialist,* Summer 1983, http://socialism.com/fs-article/cercl-zeroes-in-on-management-abuses-at-seattle-city-light/ (accessed 20 June 2018).

251 Harris, "Statement to the Media," p. 3.

252 "Notice of News Conference," issued by "women employed in diverse trades at Seattle City Light" (no date).

253 Heidi Durham, "Meeting with the Human Rights Director and Update," memo to Clara Fraser, 19 February 198[3].

254 Ibid.

255 Public statement of "complete support for our male counterparts," no date, distributed 25 February 1983.

256 Karen Meadows, et. al., letter to Mike Kelley and Charlie Silvernale, 28 February 198[3], p. 3.

257 Ibid., 2.

258 John Franklin, "Further Proposals Towards Settlement of SHR82CE029,"

memo to Joseph Recchi, 3 March 1983, p. 1.

259 Teri Bach, et al., "Content of Meeting on Monday, March 7, 1983," memo to Joe Recchi and M.J. Macdonald, 13 March 1983, p. 1.

260 IFPTE #17 organized City Light clerical workers after IBEW #77 reneged on its walkout promise to include them.

261 Joe Recchi, "Task Force on Improving the Work Environment," memo to all employees, 18 March 1983, p. 2.

262 M.J. Macdonald, "Response to Memo on the March 7 Meeting," memo to Teri Bach, et al., 30 March 1983.

263 William Hobson, Seattle Human Rights Commission, letter to Cheryl Parsons, 3 May 1983.

264 CERCL, "Labor/Community Rally Protests Discrimination at Seattle City Light," press release, 16 May 1983, p. 1.

265 Heidi Durham, "Draft of CERCL Presentation to Community Rally," 8 May 1983, p. 1.

266 CERCL, "Labor/Community Rally Protests Discrimination," p. 3.

267 Welsted, "CERCL Zeroes In on Management Abuses at Seattle City Light."

268 Ibid.

269 Ibid.

270 Teri Bach, et al., "City Light Management's Retaliation Against Supporters of the HRD Director's Complaint and CERCL's Proposals," memo to Marlaina Kiner, 29 July 1983, p. 2.

271 Kim Turner, President, AFSCME Local 2083-C, letter to Mayor Charles Royer and Superintendent Joe Recchi, 15 July 1983, p. 2.

272 Bach, et al., "City Light Management's Retaliation Against Supporters of the HRD Director's Complaint," p. 6.

273 Duff Wilson, "City Light Crews Call a Work Halt to Protest Suspension," *Seattle Post-Intelligencer,* 8 November 1983, p. C1.

274 Ibid.

275 Ibid.

276 Franklin, "Director's Employment Complaint," p. 1.

277 Ibid.

278 Ibid.

279 Ibid., p. 2–3.

280 Ibid., p. 2, 4, 5.

281 Duff Wilson, "4 Women Climb Toward Good Jobs at City Light," *Seattle Post-Intelligencer,* 28 January 1984, p. C1.

282 John Miller, "Mayoral Responsibility," KIRO-TV Commentary No. 1983-

215, 21 December 1983.

283 Kathleen Merrigan, interview by Helen Gilbert, 8 November 2017.

284 Larry Lange, "City Light Pioneer is Fired," *Seattle Post-Intelligencer*, 9 September 1988, p. B1.

285 April Branch, et al., "Verified Employment Charge," *Employee Committee for Equal Rights at City Light v. City of Seattle, City Light*, Case No. SHR83CE023, December 1983, p. 1.

286 Merrigan, interview by Hoddersen and Gilbert.

287 Merrigan, interview by Helen Gilbert.

288 Sandra Welsted, "Showdown Over Seattle's Human Rights Rollbacks," *Freedom Socialist*, Autumn 1984, http://socialism.com/fs-article/showdown-over-seattles-human-rights-rollbacks/ (accessed 22 June 2018).

289 Ibid.

290 Duff Wilson, "Royer Says He Planned to Replace Recchi Months Ago," *Seattle Post-Intelligencer*, 2 April 1984, p. A1.

291 Merrigan, interview by Hoddersen and Gilbert.

292 Margaret Norton-Arnold, "Human Relations Training: What's It All About?" *Network*, Vol. 9, No. 5, October 1984, p. 4.

293 Gamma Vision, "Progress Report: Human Relations Training for Seattle City Light," 30 August 1984, p. 3.

294 Gamma Vision, ibid., p. 3, 4.

295 Gamma Vision, ibid., p. 32.

296 Merrigan, interview by Hoddersen and Gilbert.

297 Welsted, "Showdown Over Seattle's Human Rights Rollbacks."

298 Duff Wilson, "City Light Choice May Face Hiring Policy Quiz," *Seattle Post-Intelligencer*, 12 September 1984, p. D1.

299 Lori Garrett, letter to Randall Hardy, 13 February 1985, p. 2.

300 Merrigan, interview by Hoddersen and Gilbert.

301 Ronald Fitten, "Harassed Worker Feels Vindicated," *Seattle Times*, 11 October 1996, p. B1.

302 Marilyn Endriss, Human Rights Department Enforcement Division Manager, "CERCL vs. City Light SHR 83CE023," letter to Megan Cornish, 17 April 1985.

303 (Bircher) Robeson, remarks at "A Tribute to Seattle's Pioneer Women Electricians."

304 CERCL press release, "Clara Fraser Fires Parting Salvo at City Light," 21 March 1986, p. 1–2.

305 Duff Wilson, "City Light Female Worker Reports Attack," *Seattle Post-*

Intelligencer, 29 August 1986, p. A1.

306   Ibid.

307   Clara Fraser, "Showdown Time at City Light," *Freedom Socialist,* September 1986, http://socialism.com/fs-article/showdown-time-at-city-light/ (accessed 25 June 2018).

308   Larry Works, remarks at "A Tribute to Seattle's Pioneer Women Electricians," 25th anniversary celebration hosted by Radical Women, 31 July 1999, Seattle, WA.

309   City of Seattle Public Records Request, "SCL's Apprentice Hire, Graduation and Diversity Statistics as of 12/31/2017," C013598-051917; Revised 19 January 2018.

Afterword

310   Daniel Beekman, "Discrimination Settlements Have Cost Seattle Millions, But Sexual-Harassment Data Absent," *Seattle Times,* 25 February 2018, https://www.seattletimes.com/seattle-news/politics/discrimination-settlements-have-cost-seattle-millions-but-sexual-harassment-data-absent/ (accessed 12 October 2018).

311   Larry Works, interview by Ellie Belew, 26 January 2017.

312   Jerry Lawson, interview #1 by Ellie Belew, 2 August 2016. Lawson was hired at SCL in 1981 and became one of City Light's first Black crew chiefs, working in the Underground Residential Distribution division.

313   Teri Bach, interview with Megan Cornish by Nancy Reiko Kato, 8 September 2004.

314   Aaren Thompson, interview by Ellie Belew, 11 July 2017. Thompson is a journey-level electrician constructor in Substations at Seattle City Light.

315   Sydney Brownstone, "How Sexism and Harassment Allegations at Seattle City Light Get Lost in the Dark," *The Stranger,* 8 November 2017, https://www.thestranger.com/features/2017/11/08/25547462/how-sexism-and-harassment-allegations-at-seattle-city-light-get-lost-in-the-dark (accessed 12 October 2018).

316   Seattle Silence Breakers, "Points of Unity," 9 February 2018, https://www.facebook.com/pg/seattlesilencebreakers/about/ (accessed 12 October 2018).

317   Jeff Johnson, interview by Helen Gilbert, 1 November 2018. Johnson became a journey-level worker in 1993 and is now an electrician constructor crew chief in Substations at City Light.

318   Peggy Owens, interview by Helen Gilbert, 26 September 2018. Owens started at City Light in 1996. She is a journey-level lineworker and crew chief for a line clearance crew.

319   Lawson, interview by Belew, 2 August 2016.

320   Seattle Silence Breakers, "Points of Unity."

321   Arrasmith, interview by Belew.

322   Durham, "Women with Tools," p. 2.

323   Alice Lockridge, interview by Helen Gilbert, 1 October 2018. Lockridge is active with Seattle Silence Breakers and Washington Women in Trades. She is an advocate for women in physically demanding careers.

Appendices

324   Letha Neal, *Clara Fraser v. City of Seattle,* Transcript of Hearing, Vol. 7, p. 38.

325   Patty Wong, *Clara Fraser v. City of Seattle,* Transcript of Hearing, Vol. 8, p. 140, 143.

326   Paul Boyd, "Politics and the City Light Strike," *Seattle Sun,* Vol. 3, No. 4, 28 January 1976, p. 5.

327   Charlie Silvernale, IBEW Local #77 Business Representative, interview by Ellie Belew, 10 December 2012.

328   Stan Bowen, "Local 77 Membership Goes on Strike," *The Electrical Worker,* Vol. 75, #1, p. 41.

329   Cornish, interview by Hoddersen and Gilbert.

330   John F. Kennedy, Executive Order 10925, Establishing the President's Committee on Equal Employment Opportunity, https://www.eeoc.gov/eeoc/history/35th/thelaw/eo-10925.html (accessed 11 July 2018).

331   Anne Frantilla, "Finding Aid," Human Rights Department Annual Reports, 1963-1982, http://archiveswest.orbiscascade.org/ark:/80444/xv45154 (accessed 12 July 2018).

332   William J. Clinton, "Memorandum on Affirmative Action," 19 July 1995, The American Presidency Project, http://www.presidency.ucsb.edu/ws/index.php?pid = 51632 (accessed 12 July 2018).

Index

ReD LeTTeR PReSS